baby & toddler food

baby & toddler food

Recipes and practical information for feeding babies and toddlers

Introductory text by Carol Fallows
Additional text by Karen Kingham (nutritionist)

MURDOCH BOOKS

contents

A good start to life includes a variety of tasty, healthy foods. By making an effort with your child's meals from when you start at 6 months you will establish the good habits your child will take with them into their future — a precious thing considering the number of diet-related diseases that face us in adulthood. Of course there is not always time for lengthy preparation but this does not have to be the hallmark of a good meal.

starting out

the essentials

At first you may find it hard to believe that all your precious little newborn needs for nourishment is breast milk. An amazing food and drink in one, breast milk not only provides the ultimate nutrition, it is packed with antibodies and other properties important to the health and development of your baby. Infant formula has been devised as a substitute for breast milk when breast-feeding is not possible. Specially modified to meet a baby's needs, it is the only alternative; other milks are totally unsuitable.

For the first few months all your baby will need is breast milk. Then sometime around the middle of the first year your baby will start to show an interest in food other than breast milk or formula — which will continue to remain a very important part of baby's nutrition. The guidelines for introducing your baby to family foods are not set in stone. Every baby is different and some babies will show an interest in food before 6 months and some later. A few years ago the advice of health authorities was that babies could start eating solid foods after 4 months, but it is now recommended that parents wait until closer to the 6-month mark when babies' digestive systems are able to cope with new foods and their ability to taste is developing. By this age they are also likely to have lost a reflex that makes them push out the food the moment it meets the tongue.

introducing food

It is easiest to introduce your baby to food in four stages:
1) Begin with purées. Many parents start with rice cereal, then move onto fruit and vegetable purées. Follow your baby — eating cereal as a first food is not essential.

In many other cultures weaning recipes are handed down from grandmother and mother to daughter. In Asian diets, rice is the basis of foods such as congee, which is fed to babies from around 5 months of age. At first it is sieved and mixed with lentil juice. Gradually baby will be introduced to vegetables, fresh herbs such as coriander (cilantro) and milk products such as yoghurt. In Africa, maize porridge or rice is baby's first food and in South America first foods are based on corn and potatoes.

2) After 3–5 weeks (or once your baby is happily eating puréed food from a spoon) you can introduce lumpy foods. Baby may love his rice cereal but he needs to learn about new tastes and textures. Gradually include food which has a lumpier consistency. You should also combine different foods together as well as introducing new flavours.

3) Finger foods come next. From around 8 months baby may start to show more interest in being involved in feeding. You can now add foods for chewing practice — rusks and toast are the obvious ones, but there are many more.

4) The last stage, which should have arrived by your child's first birthday, is regular food with some modifications. This means your baby will be able to eat many of the foods that the rest of the family regularly eats, with some changes and exceptions.

introducing baby to drinking from a cup

You can start to introduce your baby to a cup as early as 6 months old. If you decide to start using a cup at this age you might like to buy a baby cup that has a lid and a spout or straw. This makes it easier for you as baby is less likely to spill the contents. It will take some time for baby to get used to sucking from the cup, just as it has been for him to get used to swallowing food.

By around the age of 9 months, if you are breast-feeding and your baby has never got used to a bottle, you can go straight to the cup — and if this is the case, an ordinary plastic beaker or mug is perfectly fine; you don't have to buy a special cup. Baby needs time and opportunity to practise whatever cup he is using and he will get the hang of it. Provided you continue to offer him the breast or the bottle, he will not be thirsty while he is learning.

It is worth noting that giving a child a spout cup or a bottle to carry around most of the time is not a good idea. Children who carry these will fill up on fluid, be it water, milk or diluted juice, and even a belly full of water will stop a toddler feeling hungry at snack or meal time.

what to drink

After breast milk or formula, the most important drink for babies is water. In the first year it needs to be cooled boiled water, but once your baby reaches his first birthday, tap water is perfectly acceptable. It is worth noting that bottled water does not contain fluoride (which is important for the healthy growth of your baby's teeth) and can be high in sodium (salt). If you choose to filter your water, check that this process does not remove the fluoride.

Around 50 years ago mothers were told to introduce their babies to rose hip syrup, as it is a naturally rich source of vitamin C, at the same time as their first cereal. By the beginning of the 21st century there were dozens of 'baby' fruit juices available that contained more vitamin C than other juices, had no colourings and were usually diluted. Yet the fact remains that babies don't need rose hip syrup and they don't need juice. The main source of fluid in the first 6 months should be either breast milk or infant formula. Babies over 6 months will still enjoy breast milk or formula as their main drink, however the introduction of a cup at this time means that water, and very occasionally, diluted fruit juice, will also contribute to their total fluid intake.

reasons babies don't need juice:

- It contains fructose. Too much of this natural sugar can cause diarrhoea.
- Juice is filling — it can satisfy a baby's appetite when food or milk are more important, but it won't satisfy the body's need for nutrients.
- Too much juice can contribute to excess weight gain.
- Juice can cause tooth decay. Even diluted fruit juice can pool around baby's first teeth and cause decay. Never give your child juice at bedtime after his teeth have been cleaned.

There will come a time when your child will ask for juice and when that happens be sure to dilute it to at least 50/50. Avoid using a bottle and give it to him in a cup, but not one that he can suck from; this way it will only be a small quantity. Children between the age of one and six need no more than 1 cup of diluted juice a day. Encourage them to have a piece of fruit instead and, if they are thirsty, they can drink a cup of water.

Carbonated drinks of all kinds — even soda water added to juice or cordials — are also not suitable for babies or toddlers. Sports drinks are definitely out since they contain a cocktail of flavourings, colours and preservatives, as well as sugar, sodium and potassium and often stimulants.

your family's food

You can include shopping for baby when you shop for the family's food. Baby food sold in tins, jars or that is frozen can be expensive and baby will not learn about eating family foods if he does not eat home-made food most of the time.

Baby's nutrition needs are high so every food needs to count towards his overall nutrition needs. Foods high in sugar and fat such as chips (fries), sweet biscuits (cookies) or lollies (candy) contribute very little in the way of vitamins and minerals and take the place of foods that are more 'nutrient-dense'.

Use the following tips when you are shopping and cooking for all the family as well as for baby:

• Think fresh. It is best to have really fresh fruit and vegetables on hand. If you have a vegetable patch or fruit trees, you will have a great source of really fresh food — even a few pots of fresh herbs on the window sill will be a bonus. Shopping for fruit and vegetables every two or three days is ideal.

• Make your own. It is easy and cheaper than buying to make many of the basics such as soups and salads — and you know exactly what they contain.

• Read the labels. Some foods can contain ingredients that you would not normally suspect. For example some breakfast cereals have more salt than potato chips (crisps).

• Use little or no salt and buy low-salt products. Adults can always add salt or condiments if they find a dish needs it, but it is not possible to take it out. Babies and children do not need salt and their sense of taste is more heightened than that of adults. Cook without salt and let the adults add their own — out of sight of inquisitive little eyes.

• Don't sweeten any food with sugar or honey. Sugar is another flavour enhancer. It adds kilojoules (calories) without nourishing and can also cause tooth decay. The same goes for honey, and it is also potentially dangerous for babies under 12 months.

• Use foods that are low in animal fat — but don't give your baby or toddler low-fat foods. This may sound like a contradiction, but it isn't. The under-twos need fat in their diets, unless they are overweight (in which case they need a diet designed by a dietitian). Foods that are low in animal fat include chicken, minus the skin, lean meat and full-fat dairy products.

AGES & STAGES

BABY'S AGE	SKILLS	TYPE OF FOOD
0–6 months	Suck, suckle, swallow	Liquids
6–7 months	Begins to chew, stronger sucking ability, gag reflex disappearing	Purées
8–12 months	Bites and chews, takes all the food off a spoon, can move food in mouth	Mashes; chopped food; finger food
From 12 months on	Can move food around mouth; jaw is stronger	Family food

important nutrients

It can be worrying and confusing trying to work out if your baby is getting the right amounts of all the important nutrients he needs in order to have a healthy diet. The baby's stores of iron and zinc deplete at around the age of 6 months and milk feeds are unable to support increased requirements from this age. Commercial, iron-enriched baby rice cereals are usually one of baby's first foods and so help to top up falling iron stores.

If you introduce fruit and vegetables next, you will be giving your baby new textures and tastes as well as important vitamins and minerals; and if meat, poultry and fish follow soon after you will be ensuring that your baby receives the protein and minerals he needs. Ensuring your baby spends some time exposed to gentle indirect sunlight will provide enough vitamin D to meet his requirements.

It is now commonplace to hear that babies need vitamin supplements to ensure their intake is adequate. However, unless these have been prescribed by a doctor or a dietitian the food you are preparing and providing will give baby all the vitamins and minerals he needs. For an overview of the food sources of important nutrients, refer to the chart on pages 14–15.

There are basic guidelines you can follow that will help to ensure you are meeting baby's nutritional needs. These are:

- breast-feed
- provide a variety of nutritious foods
- avoid low-fat diets
- be careful not to over or underfeed
- offer water as the first drink
- do not add sugar to baby's food
- choose low-salt foods and do not add salt to baby's food
- serve foods that contain calcium
- serve foods that contain iron

including nutrients

There are many practical ways to ensure important nutrients are included in your family's diet, such as:

- Eating a wide range of breads, including wholegrain and wholemeal (whole-wheat), and plenty of cereals, rice, pasta and noodles. From these foods come fibre, vitamins, minerals, carbohydrates and protein.
- Choosing a wide variety of fresh vegetables and legumes. Tinned and frozen are an alternative when fresh are not available. Important vitamins, minerals, dietary fibre and carbohydrate are found in vegetables, beans, lentils

and legumes. When planning a family meal a simple way to include a wide variety of vitamins and minerals is to think one white, one red or yellow and one green vegetable.

• Eating plenty of fruit and choosing whole fruit instead of fruit juice. Dried fruits are a nutritious alternative, as are tinned and frozen fruit without any added sugar. Fruit provides vitamins, including vitamin C and folate, carbohydrates and fibre.

• Offering milk, yoghurt and cheese, all of which are valuable sources of calcium, protein, riboflavin and vitamin B12. You don't have to drink milk and eat cheese — you can add milk to soups, casseroles and sauces; include cheese in dishes such as omelettes and vegetable dishes; and use yoghurt in curries and dips. Low- and reduced-fat dairy products are not suitable for babies and toddlers under the age of 2 years. Other sources of calcium include tinned fish, soy milk, lentils, almonds, brazil nuts and dried apricots.

• Including a variety of lean meat, fish, poultry, eggs and legumes in the diet. These foods provide protein, iron and zinc; and red meat is particularly high in these nutrients. Nuts are also an important source of these nutrients, but whole nuts must never be given to children under 5 because they are a choking hazard. Smooth nut butters or crushed nuts are fine for children to consume, as long as they don't have a nut allergy.

• If you are vegetarian, legumes, seeds and nuts as well as wholegrain cereals and breads are important and need to be eaten at the same meal as fruit in order to maximize the absorption of important minerals such as iron.

the vegetarian or vegan baby

Families who do not eat meat will often want their babies to follow the same diet as they do. Vegetarian babies can be weaned in much the same way as babies whose families eat meat. Milk, cheese and eggs will provide first-class animal protein. Dried beans, peas, lentils and ground nuts are good sources of vegetable protein. As you do with your own diet, if you are vegetarian you will soon begin to combine vegetable protein with whole-grain cereals in order to get a complete protein. For example, you might combine soya beans with brown rice, or wholemeal (whole-wheat) bread with peanut butter. Fruit and vegetables will be a good source of many of the important nutrients and cereals and green vegetables will provide iron, which will be more useful as a nutrient when it is combined with a vitamin C-rich food. A vegan diet cannot provide all the nutrients a baby or toddler needs and is not recommended for small children. Refer to the chart on the following pages for the sources of important nutrients.

SOURCES OF MAJOR NUTRIENTS

NUTRIENT	FOOD SOURCES	IMPORTANT FOR
Protein	Breast milk, infant formula, lean meats, fish, seafood, poultry, eggs, dairy foods, legumes, grains, nuts, seeds	Growth and repair of all body cells. Children have a proportionally greater need for protein than adults because they are growing and protein is needed for the formation of new cells
Fat	Breast milk, infant formula, oils, margarine, lean meats, fish, eggs, dairy foods, whole grains, olives, avocados, nuts, seeds	General health and the absorption of fat-soluble vitamins A, D, E and K. Fats are also an important stored source of energy/fuel for growing babies and toddlers. This is because of their small stomachs and high needs for energy
Essential fatty acids (omega-3 fats)	Breast milk, some infant formula, lean meats, fish, canola, sunflower and safflower oils and margarine, linseeds (flax seeds), walnuts, pecans, egg yolk	Brain and visual development, plus the production of hormone-like substances. Unlike other fats, these can't be made by the body so must come from food
Carbohydrates	Breast milk, infant formula, grains such as wheat, rice, oats, barley and the foods made from them such as bread, pasta, breakfast cereals, flour, semolina. Sugar, sweet corn, potato, root vegetables, fruit, milk	Supplying the body with its major source of energy. In their unprocessed forms, they are good sources of fibre
Fibre	Wholegrain breads and cereals, vegetables, fruits, legumes (dried peas and beans), nuts, seeds	Healthy, regular functioning bowel
Vitamin A (retinol)	Breast milk, infant formula, dairy foods, liver, eggs, fortified margarine, oily fish	Well developed vision and healthy skin and hair
Beta-carotene	Orange and green fruit and vegetables such as sweet potatoes, carrots, orange-fleshed melon, apricots, spinach, broccoli	Supply of vitamin A (beta-carotenes are converted into vitamin A in the body)
Thiamin (vitamin B1)	Breast milk, infant formula, wheat germ and wholemeal (whole-wheat) foods such as breads and cereals, yeast extracts, nuts, fortified breakfast cereals, lean pork	Release of energy from carbohydrate foods
Riboflavin (vitamin B2)	Breast milk, infant formula, dairy products, yeast extracts, meat extracts, eggs, fortified breakfast cereals, mushrooms, wholemeal (whole-wheat) flour and bread	Healthy skin and eyes and the release of energy from food

SOURCES OF MAJOR NUTRIENTS

NUTRIENT	FOOD SOURCES	IMPORTANT FOR
Niacin (vitamin B3)	Breast milk, infant formula, lean meats, peanuts, fish, legumes, fortified breakfast cereals, eggs, milk	Growth and release of energy from food
Vitamin B12	Breast milk, infant formula, lean meats, chicken, fish, seafood, eggs, milk, fortified vegetarian products	Formation of nerve cells, genetic material (DNA) and red blood cells
Folic acid	Breast milk, infant formula, green leafy vegetables, whole grains, legumes, nuts, fortified breakfast cereals	Healthy growth; development; formation of red blood cells
Vitamin C	Breast milk, infant formula, potato, parsley, brussels sprouts, cabbage, capsicum (pepper), citrus fruits and juices, mango, berries, papaya	Healthy skin, bone and gums; helps the body absorb iron from foods other than meat
Vitamin D	Breast milk, infant formula, oily fish, eggs, butter, margarine, cheese	Absorption of calcium and phosphorus and for strong and healthy teeth and bones. The body also makes this vitamin in the skin when it is exposed to sunlight
Vitamin E	Breast milk, infant formula, wheat germ and wheat germ oil, nuts, seeds and the oils of nuts and seeds	Development and maintenance of healthy body cells — especially in the blood and nervous systems, due to its antioxidant properties
Iron	Breast milk, lean meats, chicken, fish, eggs, legumes, fortified baby cereals, wholegrain cereals, dark green leafy vegetables, dried fruits	Healthy blood and muscles. It is estimated that more than one in three young children don't receive their recommended needs for iron*
Calcium	Breast milk, infant formula, dairy foods, calcium-fortified soy products, tinned sardines and salmon (including bones)	Growth of strong and healthy bones and teeth. Almost 50 per cent of toddlers don't get enough of this mineral*
Fluoride	Fluoridated drinking water, fish	Strengthening teeth and reducing the risk of dental decay. Although not essential, the inclusion of fluoride in the diet is recommended by the World Health Organization (WHO)
Zinc	Breast milk, infant formula, lean meat, chicken, seafood, milk, legumes, nuts	Healthy growth, wound healing and immune system. Young children often don't get enough of this mineral

Statistics from the 1995 Australian National Nutrition Survey

genetically modified food

Genetic modification of food has been around for centuries with the selective breeding of animals and food crops, but the genetically modified (GM) foods of today include ingredients that have been modified by gene technology. This has enabled many crops to be modified to make them resistant to insects and viruses and more tolerant to herbicides. Crops that have been modified in some countries include soya bean, rape seed (canola), chicory, corn, squash and potato and genetically modified food ingredients are present in some foods. Soy flour in bread, for example, may have come from modified soya beans. In some countries food labels are required by law to show if a food has been genetically modified and this may apply to baby food. While there are distinct advantages to GM foods in increased quality and quantity of food with longer shelf life, their safety is still being debated. It is impossible to predict all the potential effects, including the risks.

Making food for your baby and toddler at home means that if you want to you can avoid GM foods by being selective about which products you include in your shopping.

organic food

Organic foods have been produced without the use of synthetic fertilizers, pesticides or other chemicals. They are not genetically modified and irradiation is prohibited. Only free-range animals are can be considered organic. When a food is organically certified it means that not only has it been organically grown but also harvested, prepared and transported using systems that guarantee the produce is not contaminated by synthetic chemicals.

Organic baby food is one of the biggest growth areas for organic farmers in many countries.

When you prepare your own food you know exactly what the ingredients are and how it has been prepared. You can buy commercial baby foods that are organically certified. However, you need to be aware that these foods may contain small amounts of non-organic ingredients and these will be specified on the label.

For families on a tight budget organic food can be expensive. Much organic food is more expensive than regular food because it costs more to produce. Looking for bargains, using your freezer, buying food when it is in season, buying frozen organic vegetables if they are cheaper than the non-frozen variety, growing some of your own food and creating a compost heap or worm farm are some of the ways you can provide your family with a diet based on organic foods.

FOOD TYPE	DANGER
Honey (under 12 months)	Honey can contain botulism spores which can cause serious health problems in babies — fortunately this is rare. It is not known why this only affects babies under the age of 12 months, but older children and adults are not affected. You should also not include honey in any cooking for babies under the age of 12 months
Tea, coffee or herbal teas	Tea and coffee, including decaffeinated coffee and some herbal teas, contain caffeine. Herbal teas can also contain other substances not suitable for children
Raw or undercooked eggs	Egg allergy is most common in babies under the age of 12 months. Cooked eggs are better tolerated
Nuts	Children cannot chew whole nuts such as peanuts. It is possible for children to choke on or inhale whole nuts. It is therefore advised that children do not eat whole nuts until they are 5 years old. They can eat smooth nut butters or crushed nuts if they are not allergic to them
Hard foods	Young children can easily choke on foods such as raw and cooked peas, raw carrot, popcorn, hard cheese chunks, large pieces of raw apple, lollies (candy), whole nuts and whole grapes
Cow's milk (under 12 months) and soy beverages (under 2 years)	These are poor sources of iron and should not be substituted for breast milk or formula in the first 12 months. They can be added to foods in cooking. Both are potential allergens. Their use as a main drink is acceptable from 12 months for cow's milk and from 2 years for soy beverages
Snack foods	Babies need maximum nutrition because every food counts and these foods are high in kilojoules (calories) but low on nutrition
Soft drinks or alcohol	Soft drinks offer no nutritional benefits and can affect a child's growth and ability to gain weight. Alcohol is totally unsuitable and must never be given to a child
Raw or uncooked meat products	Delicatessen meats such as salami are not suitable for babies or children

foods to take care with:

soy milk: Unless a soy milk infant formula has been prescribed for your baby or toddler because of an intolerance to lactose (the natural sugar found in breast milk and cow's milk), it is not a recommended food for your child. Soy milks and drinks which are not specially designed for babies must not be given to a baby, and are not suitable as a drink for children under 2 years old.

These soy milks are not a complete food and do not have enough iron, calcium or vitamins to be a substitute for breast milk or infant formula. They also do not contain vitamin B12 (an essential vitamin for growth and development), they are too rich in minerals and they have too much protein, but not the protein containing essential amino acids that growing children need (these are added to soy infant formula).

Soy milk and soy milk formulas have a natural aluminium content that is higher than cow's milk, cow's milk formula or breast milk. Soy products also contain phyto-oestrogens. Though many babies have been consuming soy milk formula for some years it is not known what the long-term effects might be. So unless your baby has a diagnosed intolerance to dairy products it is best to offer dairy milk products instead until he is at least 2 years old, when soy can be introduced as part of a varied diet.

cow's milk: Breast milk is of course ideal at any time, though take care not to overheat expressed breast milk as important nutrients and immune factors can be destroyed. For the first 12 months, breast milk or a cow's milk-based infant formula is the ideal milk for your child to drink, but you can include cow's milk in cooking or yoghurt or custard after about 7 months. Cow's milk, as a regular drink, is too high in sodium for baby's kidneys. Cow's milk, goat's milk and sheep's milk are very poor sources of iron and also lack many of the other important nutrients — including vitamins A, C and E — that are found in breast milk and which are added to infant formulas; they are not suitable for babies in the first year. Unpasteurized milk from any animal can carry salmonella which causes food poisoning, so it should never be given to babies or toddlers.

eggs: Eggs are a very good food. If your family has no history of allergy such as eczema or asthma, you can introduce egg yolk to your baby's diet from around the age of 8 months. Egg white can be added a month or two later, if there were no problems with the egg yolk. There is no research to suggest that cholesterol is a problem at this age. It is better not to give undercooked or raw eggs to children before they are 1 year old.

healthy not fat

It is estimated that between 25 and 30 per cent of children under the age of 5 are overweight — some of these are obese. Some health experts are classing obesity as an epidemic because there are so many related health problems. How and what you feed your baby in the early years will determine whether he has a weight problem. Babies who are breast-fed have the best start — they are less likely to become obese and babies who are breast-fed for a year or longer are five times less likely to be obese than babies who are not; babies who are breast-fed for 3–5 months are half as likely to be overweight when they are older.

how to ensure your baby is fit and healthy — and not fat:

• Don't introduce solid foods before baby is ready. Ideally solid food should not introduced before 6 months of age.

• Stick to small portions of food — if baby doesn't want to eat, don't force it. Keep meal times relaxed and let your child decide how much he will and won't eat, being sure to provide healthy choices at all times.

• Don't introduce sugary, fatty or fast foods at all. One day someone will give your child something you would rather he didn't have, like a doughnut or hot chips (fries) — but until then, avoid these foods.

• Never give your baby or toddler soft drinks. Make milk and water the main drinks and water down drinks of juice to at least 50/50.

• Give your baby or child the space to exercise. From the time he is crawling, he needs to practise using his muscles as much as possible. Once he can walk he will love running and playing outdoors. Family exercise, such as ball games, walking to the shops, trips to the park or the beach ideally should happen every day.

commercial baby food

Baby food in tins or jars or that is frozen can be a saviour when you are in a hurry, things are not going to plan, you have to go out or you are away from home, but it is best saved for these times and not given to your baby every day.

Unlike foods you prepare at home, commercial baby food is of a very uniform consistency. Purées are smooth regardless of the vegetable from which they are made and different from what you would prepare at home. The smoothness of puréed pumpkin (winter squash) is nothing like the grainy texture of puréed broccoli or green peas and it is these subtle differences in foods that help to prepare baby for the stages to come.

Commercial foods for older toddlers have similar problems. Though they may have lumps, the type of cooking they are subjected to makes them very soft, offering little resistance and variation in texture compared to that provided by a mashed home-cooked food.

Taste is another factor to consider. Try the food you offer your baby and you will soon discover that with some brands chicken and vegetable tastes much the same as beef and vegetable and probably has little similarity to something that would come from your own kitchen.

Using your own home-prepared meals also means you know exactly what your baby or toddler is eating. While this may still be the case for high-quality commercial baby foods which provide ingredient lists with percentage amounts for each ingredient, others don't and can 'pad out' the contents with extra water and thickeners. It is not unknown to find only 10 per cent chicken in a chicken baby food which leaves you wondering what the rest of the meal contains.

Thickeners are not necessarily a bad thing for babies and toddlers and are usually needed to hold a product together and stop it from separating. It is when they are used to take the place of 'real' ingredients that the nutrition of the meal becomes diluted.

Once your baby moves on to toddler food there exists another range of commercial foods designed to make your life easier. As with baby foods, they can be a great convenience when time is short. However, unlike baby foods which have very strict guidelines about what can be added to them, food for toddlers don't have the same restrictions. Avoid toddler foods that use too much salt, added sugar or contain flavours and preservatives.

Generally, toddlers don't need to eat specially formulated and marketed children's food. Provided you are choosing healthy convenience options for the whole family they can eat what you are eating.

For more information on how to get the best for your baby and toddler ready prepared and off the shelf, check the section on reading labels (page 21).

quick meal solutions

Trying to feed hungry young children and babies when they want food that very instant is never easy. Think of the quick options you might already have to hand:

• Team mashed fruits with a spoonful of ricotta cheese or thick plain yoghurt for a more nourishing meal.

• No-added-salt or reduced-salt baked beans and creamed corn are excellent stand-by meals; serve them with toast fingers for older toddlers.

• Reduced-salt or water-packed tinned fish (salmon, tuna, sardines, mackerel) all mash and flake really well — just crush or remove any bones (which are usually very soft anyway).

• Avocado, banana, mango, papaya, pear or kiwi fruit take very little time to prepare and no cooking.

• It also takes no time at all to beat an egg and make an omelette — see our recipe for this basic and nourishing meal on page 70.

read the label!

A lot can be learned from reading the ingredients list on a product's label. The ingredient in the greatest quantity will come first and so on down to the last ingredient. If you find ingredients that you wouldn't normally put into your own version of a baby food, such as ground rice or other cereals, it is likely they are being used to bulk the meal out so consider another brand. You should also consider the following:

• If the food's name is based on ingredients such as 'sweet corn and chicken', then the manufacturer is obliged to state what percentage these ingredients are of the final food. High-quality baby foods will do this with all their ingredients so you know exactly what you are feeding your baby.

• In most countries the information panel will tell you about the energy, fat, protein, carbohydrate, sugar and sodium content of the food 'per serve' and/or 'per 100 g'. Using the 'per 100 g' column, if it is present, makes comparing food products easy. Other nutrients may also be on the panel but those listed above will usually always be there. For more information on food labels and how to use them contact your local government food authority.

• When shopping for young children consider the amount of sodium and sugar in food. As well, fat might be an issue for the family as a whole, but low-fat foods are not appropriate for young children

• Sodium is part of sodium chloride or salt. Many commercial foods can be high in salt. The easiest way to keep salt to a minimum in your family's diet is to look for products labelled no-added-salt, reduced-salt or low-salt. The other way is to compare products and choose the one with the lowest amount of sodium. As a guide, a low-salt food will have a sodium content of about 120 milligrams (mg) per 100 g or around 6 per cent of your recommended daily value (RDA) per serve.

• Sugar is not bad for children when it comes to them naturally, as it does in fruit and milk. You can keep extra sugar out of your family's diet by choosing foods with no-added-sugar, reduced-sugar or low-in-sugar on the label.

Because sugar might occur naturally from fruit-based ingredients, using your judgement based on the ingredients list and the nutrition label is often best. For example, it is unlikely a fruit-based food will ever be labelled 'low sugar', but this doesn't mean that it won't be healthy if it has no added sugars and just contains the natural sugars from the fruit.

• 'No artificial colours, flavours or preservatives' is something that you may find on the labels of food marketed for children. Be aware that it is not only the artificial ones that can cause problems for children. That said, the majority of the additives used in the world's food supply are necessary to ensure food is safe for us to eat. If you are concerned about additives in your child's diet see the allergy and intolerance section in this book (page 198) for information.

food safety

Bacteria and viruses can cause food-borne illness in children and adults and it is not always possible to tell by the way food looks, smells or tastes whether it contains pathogens. Being careful and hygienic will help you to prevent food poisoning which can be a very serious illness in babies. This care begins when you shop for food.

• Shop for non-perishables first and put cold foods in an insulated container.
• Put raw meats in separate bags from other foods.
• Do not buy foods in damaged packaging.
• Avoid chilled food or frozen food that are stacked high in cabinets, since they may have been there for some time.
• Be sure that staff at the delicatessen counter are using separate tongs for each food and wearing gloves to handle food. Ask for meats to be cut freshly.
• Only buy hot foods if you will be home in half an hour, then reheat the food as soon as you arrive home, or refrigerate it.
• Refrigerate all cold foods as soon as you arrive home.
• Unpack perishables straight away.
• Before you do anything in the kitchen and in between tasks wash your hands in warm soapy water.
• Cover cooked food.
• Cool hot food quickly — put it into the refrigerator as soon as the steam has stopped rising.
• Make sure your refrigerator is between 4–5°C (39–41°F); and your freezer is between 15–18°C (59–65°F).
• Thaw frozen food in the refrigerator or microwave rather than on the kitchen bench or chopping board.
• Do not prepare family food if you have vomiting or diarrhoea.

- Use separate chopping boards and utensils for cooked and raw foods and wash them in hot soapy water.
- Be sure the food you cook is completely cooked through. This is particularly important for poultry and minced (ground) meat — juices should run clear when poultry is pierced with a skewer.
- Always reheat food to steaming hot. If you are using a microwave be sure to stir the food during reheating — and if it is for baby, taste it with a separate spoon. It is not recommended that you heat a baby's bottle in the microwave because of the way the milk heats unevenly.
- Don't use the same plate for raw and cooked food.
- Thoroughly wash and dry all fruit and vegetables.
- Wash all working surfaces with warm soapy water.
- Change tea towels (dish towels) and dishcloths regularly — every couple of days at least. Disposable paper towels are a good alternative.
- Wash baby's hands before — and after — he eats.
- Never mix pet dishes with your own — wash and dry them separately.

babies with colic

When a baby cries uncontrollably and seems irritable and uncomfortable the diagnosis is usually colic. There is no one cause for colic and in most cases a cause cannot be determined. By the time a baby is ready to start eating solid foods he has usually outgrown colic. There is no reason to give solid food early in an attempt to relieve the condition. As baby's gut matures he will outgrow the colic.

babies with reflux

Reflux (gastro-oesophogeal reflux) is one of the most common problems that can make feeding difficult. Most babies bring up a little food at some stage, and some do it after every feed. This is not reflux, it is called possetting. Possetting is perfectly normal and as your baby's digestive system matures it will stop. Reflux is more serious and can be mild or severe. A baby with reflux will either vomit easily and often or be very distressed after a feed because he is in pain. This pain is caused by acid from the stomach irritating the oesophagus, which is the tube that connects the mouth with the stomach. Children with reflux usually grow out of it between 6 and 18 months of age.

If your child is distressed after feeds, vomits frequently or in large amounts, or if there is blood present, and he is not gaining weight you need to talk to your doctor.

	1 MONTH	2 MONTHS	3 MONTHS	4 MONTHS	5 MONTHS	6 MONTHS
Breast milk and/or infant formula	All baby needs in the first 6 months is breast milk, no other solids or fluids. If breast milk is not available offer infant formula					Offer breast milk or formula before food
Cereals and bread						Baby rice cereal, steamed rice
Fruits & vegetables						Cooked/stewed apple, pear, pumpkin (squash), potato, sweet potato. Fresh avocado, banana
Meat, chicken, fish, egg, legumes, lentils and tofu						
Dairy products						
AMOUNTS / TEXTURE	Breast milk or formula according to baby's need					1–2 teaspoons puréed

7 MONTHS	8 MONTHS	9 MONTHS	10 MONTHS	11 MONTHS	12 MONTHS	13+ MONTHS
	Introduce cooled boiled water as an occasional drink from a regular rimmed or spouted cup		Offer breast milk after food	Continue to offer breast milk. Aim to breastfeed for at least 12 months — 2 years is ideal		
	Other baby cereals, oats, corn, pasta, couscous, polenta	Unsweetened adult cereals, wholemeal (whole-wheat) and wholegrain breads, unsalted crackers			Include baby in family foods and snacks, starting with very small amounts	
Gradually introduce a wide variety of fruits and vegetables. Melon, peaches, plums, apricot, papaya, beans, broccoli, carrot, zucchini (courgette), parsnip, cauliflower		Offer water as the main drink in addition to breast milk or formula. Fruit juice should be diluted to at least 50/50 and only offered occasionally and never in a bottle, only in a cup			Avoid offering fruit cordials and soft drinks, limit fruit juices to half a diluted cup per day	
Chicken, lamb, fish, beef, legumes, lentils, tofu	Egg yolk (cooked)		Whole egg (cooked)			Nuts, crushed or as smooth butters
Full-fat plain yoghurt, custard, mild cheddar cheese, small amounts of cow's milk if cooked						Full-cream cow's milk as a drink. If still breast-feeding less cow's milk needed
2–4 tablespoons, increasing according to baby's needs. Mashed soft food and finger foods		2–4 tablespoons according to baby's needs. Grated, minced (ground) and finely chopped.			Vary textures and quantities according to baby's appetite. Offer a variety of foods in small amounts.	

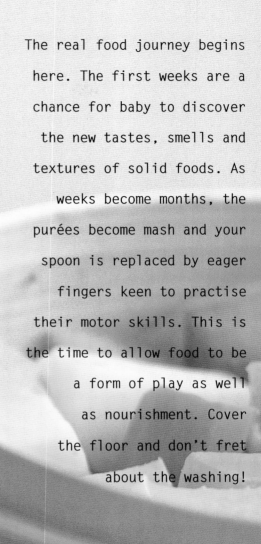

The real food journey begins here. The first weeks are a chance for baby to discover the new tastes, smells and textures of solid foods. As weeks become months, the purées become mash and your spoon is replaced by eager fingers keen to practise their motor skills. This is the time to allow food to be a form of play as well as nourishment. Cover the floor and don't fret about the washing!

baby food

first foods

Obviously, you want your baby to enjoy eating, and also to enjoy meal times. It is important, therefore, that you don't force your baby to take solids if she is not yet ready for them; this makes meal times difficult. Instead, keep feeding your baby the usual amounts of nourishing breast milk or infant formula until she exhibits the signs that she is ready.

In the early days, food is a new learning experience and your baby is still getting all her vitamins, minerals and protein from milk, while the new foods are providing valuable kilojoules (calories). The main aim in the early days is to avoid foods that could cause allergies. Theoretically you can feed your baby almost any food that you are eating, if you avoid those that could cause an allergic reaction, and which baby likes the taste of and which is the right consistency — a purée or liquid. Most people, however, start their baby on a cereal, often rice, as these are less likely to cause an allergic reaction than a wheat cereal.

some signs baby may be ready for solids:

- Baby holds things and puts them in her mouth. She may try to grab food you are eating. If the food is bland you can test her readiness by dipping a clean finger into it and letting her suck off the food. If she enjoys it, try her out with some rice cereal.
- Baby is able to sit supported and hold her head up.
- She has lost the tongue-thrust reflex. If the moment a spoon or your finger touches baby's tongue it 'thrusts' the spoon or finger out, then baby is not ready. This reflex is important as it protects a baby from choking.
- Baby seems to still be hungry after a milk feed and is not gaining weight. Younger babies will go through periods, usually at around 6 weeks and 3–4 months, when they seem to be hungry after feeding, but this can be solved by offering them more breast milk or formula.

don't feed baby before she's ready because:

- It won't make her sleep better or sleep through the night. That happens with maturity. Babies need to learn to sleep at night.

- She is more likely to develop allergies as her system is not mature enough to cope with food other than milk.
- She is susceptible to infections or tummy upsets.
- She may not drink as much breast milk or formula as she needs for optimum growth.
- Constipation is more likely as her system cannot cope with solids yet.
- If you feed solids too early, feeding can be a messy business, especially with a baby who has not lost the tongue-thrust reflex. Why make more work for yourself and baby?

how baby learns to swallow

Up until now baby has only needed to suck to get the sustenance she needs. Now she must learn that nourishment also comes from food and to do this she must learn to swallow and chew as well. Watching you eat, sitting at the table while others eat and being able to touch, finger and play with food is all part of this learning process. Baby needs time to learn these new skills so make her first feeds at a time when she is not ravenous. If baby regularly falls asleep after a milk feed you may find that the best time for other foods is in the middle of the milk feed.

When you first put food on baby's tongue she won't know what to do with it. She may move it around until much of it dribbles out of her mouth. You can't overcome this by putting the food at the back of her mouth, as this may cause her to gag. One method that often works is to allow your baby to simply suck it off the spoon. Using this method will help you to know when baby has had enough because she will usually turn her head away or close her lips.

making life easy

When you prepare baby's food do so in batches and freeze it — this cuts down on the preparation time needed for the next time you make the meal. Make enough baby food to fill up half an ice cube tray — each cube is around 1 tablespoon. When you have done this a few times with a variety of different purées, you will have a well-stocked range of foods that you can thaw easily and mix together.

When you thaw and reheat baby food make sure it is very hot, then cool it down — if you are using the microwave, stir the food before you test it on the inside of your wrist. Like formula, left-over baby food must be discarded because it will contain bacteria-carrying saliva. Never re-freeze it or store it for later use.

from 6 months

When first introducing solids to your baby, choose a time of day that suits you best. It might be after breakfast or before dinner, but you need to have time to take it gently and slowly. Over the next month you will introduce other meal times.

Always give baby her milk before you offer other foods — milk is still the most important source of nutrition for baby; it will not be replaced by food for another couple of months.

For her first meal offer her 1 teaspoon of one food, for example rice cereal. If she enjoys this, you can mix up another teaspoon for her next 'meal'. You can mix the cereal with expressed breast milk, formula or cooled boiled water. Remember, her first feed needs to have a runny consistency.

Use a clean bowl and spoon. Be sure to wash baby's bowls and cutlery in hot soapy water and to rinse thoroughly before drying with a clean tea towel (dish towel), if you don't have a dishwasher. Start by feeding baby on your lap which is covered with a towel or a nappy (diaper) and be prepared for a mess. You can move to a highchair when you think baby is ready.

After a couple of days with one food, try a new food. In the beginning it is important to offer new foods one at a time so baby can learn about different tastes and textures and you can determine if there are any foods that do not agree with baby. If baby does not like a particular food, try another and try again at a later date.

Don't add any salt or sugar — even if the food tastes bland or tasteless to you. Babies have 'new' tastebuds that taste flavours much more sharply than adults.

Once baby is eating solids you will notice a change to the smell of her urine and the look and smell of her bowel movements. Also any possetting (see page 23) will have a stronger smell. If your baby has been breast-fed until now, the change to the smell will be more noticeable as breast milk does not cause the strong smells that formula does.

After a couple of weeks baby will have tried a few new foods and you can mix them together for variety. Baby has to learn that food can be as satisfying as milk — she does not know this yet. You may find that sometimes baby will cry because she is hungry but giving her purée does not seem to work. It may be because she didn't have her milk feed first.

ground rice cereal

Rice cereal (either home-made or ready-made) is the best food to begin with because it is one of the foods least likely to cause an adverse reaction.

40 g (1½ oz/¼ cup) short-grain polished rice

125 ml (4 fl oz/½ cup) water

Prep time: 5 minutes
Cooking time: 5 minutes
Makes 6 serves

Grind the rice to a smooth powder in a spice grinder or use a mortar and pestle.

Put in a small saucepan and stir in the water. Stir over low heat for 2–3 minutes, or until the mixture becomes thick and creamy.

bulk rice cereal

Grind 220 g (7¾ oz/1 cup) short-grain polished rice to a smooth powder in a spice grinder or in a mortar with a pestle. Put in a small saucepan and stir in 625 ml (21½ fl oz/2½ cups) water. Stir over low heat for 2–3 minutes, or until the mixture becomes thick and creamy. Pour into ice cube trays and freeze.

puréed vegetable

Try pumpkin (winter squash) as a first vegetable for your baby. Its smooth, creamy texture and naturally sweet flavour make it enjoyable for new palates.

150 g (5½ oz/½ cup) vegetable such as finely chopped pumpkin (winter squash), potato, carrot, sweet potato, parsnip, peas, English spinach, broccoli or zucchini (courgette)

breast milk, formula or cooled boiled water

Prep time: 5 minutes
Cooking time: 15 minutes
Makes 6–8 serves

Put the chosen vegetable into a steamer basket over a saucepan of gently simmering water. Cover tightly and steam until tender.

Finely purée the vegetable pieces with a fork or press through a sieve. Add a little breast milk, formula or cooled boiled water to the mixture to achieve a smooth consistency.

After feeding, spoon the (untouched) remainder into ice cube trays and freeze or store in the refrigerator for up to 3 days.

variation: If using tomatoes, peel and deseed them before passing them through a fine sieve.

puréed avocado

Rich in healthy monounsaturated fats, avocado is also a good source of vitamin E and many of the B vitamins. This good nutrition, combined with its smooth, easy-to-prepare texture, means you have a perfect first food for babies.

Choose a small, soft avocado. Mash or purée one-eighth of the avocado with breast milk, formula or cooled boiled water to achieve the desired consistency.

stewed fruit

Babies are born with an innate taste for sweet foods; the natural sweetness of fresh stewed fruits makes them great favourites with babies.

1 medium apple, peach or pear, peeled, cored and sliced

Prep time: 5 minutes
Cooking time: 5 minutes
Makes 6–8 serves

Put the sliced fruit into a small saucepan with 2 tablespoons water. Bring to the boil, reduce the heat and simmer until soft and pulpy, adding more water as required.

Purée with a little boiled water to make about 125 ml (4 fl oz/½ cup) stewed fruit.

variations: You can also use a variety of other fruits such as rhubarb or peeled and cored plums or apricots.

mashed banana

Bananas are rich in vitamin C, an important nutrient to help boost baby's iron absorption.

Choose a ripe banana. Mash or purée the banana with breast milk, formula or cooled boiled water to achieve the desired consistency.

pear & sweet potato purée

Once baby has tried a range of single fruits and vegetables, expand her repertoire. Combine fruits, vegetables and even rice cereal to create a new food experience.

80 g (2¾ oz/⅔ cup) chopped sweet potato

80 g (2¾ oz/⅔ cup) peeled, cored and chopped pear

breast milk, formula or cooled boiled water

Prep time: 5 minutes

Cooking time: 12 minutes

Makes 1–2 serves

Put the chopped sweet potato and pear pieces in a steamer basket over a saucepan of gently simmering water. Cover tightly and steam for about 12 minutes, or until very tender.

Finely purée the pieces with a fork or press through a sieve. Add a little breast milk, formula or cooled boiled water to the mixture to achieve a smooth consistency.

After feeding, spoon the (untouched) remainder into ice cube trays and freeze or store in the refrigerator for up to 3 days.

COMBINATION IDEAS:

• *Parsnip and carrot*

• *Baby pea and apple*

• *Avocado and pear*

• *Broccoli, carrot and potato*

• *Dried apricot and rice cereal*

• *Avocado and ricotta cheese (from 7 months)*

• *Potato and leek*

• *Pumpkin (winter squash) and apple*

• *Broccoli and sweet potato*

The combinations are only limited by your imagination!

from 7 months

Once baby is used to eating from a spoon, has tried a few different purées and is having two or three feeds a day, it is time to start making the food more lumpy. This stage usually comes around 7–8 months.

Don't worry if she doesn't have any teeth. Babies have very hard gums, as any breastfeeding mother will know, and are able to chew. If baby doesn't start eating mashed food at this stage, her cheek and jaw muscles will not get the workout they need and it will be more difficult when she is older.

a growing apetite

Though milk is still important, you may like to start giving food before the milk and start getting into more of a routine for meal times. Breast milk or formula can be given when baby wakes up and for morning, afternoon and evening 'snacks'.

Baby is growing quite quickly and you may find her appetite is growing too. She may be having around 2 tablespoons or she may be hungry enough to eat around half a cup of food. Never force baby to eat. It is better to have too little food and have to make her something else than to feel unhappy that baby has not eaten all the food you have prepared so carefully.

You can start giving your baby finger foods sometime soon. Babies love rusks (home-made or ready-made). Even if they are not teething, babies enjoy chomping on them. Foods which dissolve easily when they are sucked or chewed make ideal finger foods — foods which are bitten off in hard lumps (such as carrot, apple or celery) do not, because of the possibility of choking.

At this age baby will be able to sit up and will enjoy sitting in a high chair or a hook-on chair. She will enjoy eating with you sometimes — try to do this at least once a day since she will learn a great deal about eating and food by eating with the family.

Expect a mess. Learning about texture does not just happen with the tongue. When baby plays with her food she is also learning about food and, maybe surprisingly, some of it will end up in her mouth. Some babies are strongly independent and want to feed themselves everything. The best way around this is to have two spoons, one for baby and one for you.

Don't feel that in order to be a good parent you need to make all baby's food. Ready-made baby foods can make a great stand-by, and are useful when you are out and about. They are also hygienic and can provide good nutrition.

baby oat porridge

Oats provide all the goodness of a whole grain, as well as giving baby long-lasting energy throughout the day. Oats are also an excellent source of fibre.

25 g (1 oz/¼ cup) rolled (porridge) oats

185 ml (6 fl oz/¾ cup) milk

Prep time: 5 minutes

Cooking time: 5 minutes

Makes 3–4 serves

Grind the rolled oats to a fine powder in a spice grinder or a small food processor.

Put the oats in a small saucepan and gradually whisk in the milk and 60 ml (2 fl oz/¼ cup) water until well combined. Slowly bring to the boil and cook for 1–2 minutes, stirring constantly, or until the mixture thickens. Remove from the heat.

cauliflower soup

Cauliflower, along with broccoli, brussels sprouts and cabbage, belongs to the Brassica family of vegetables, which are all excellent sources of vitamin C.

2 teaspoons olive oil

1 small onion, chopped

1 small garlic clove, crushed (optional)

300 g (10½ oz/2½ cups) cauliflower, cut into small florets

500 ml (17 fl oz/2 cups) salt-reduced vegetable or chicken stock

Prep time: 10 minutes

Cooking time: 15 minutes

Makes 6–8 serves

Heat the oil in a saucepan over medium heat. Add the onion and garlic and cook for 2–3 minutes, or until softened. Add the cauliflower and stock, cover and bring to the boil. Reduce the heat to low and simmer for 10 minutes. Cool slightly and process in a blender or food processor until smooth.

The soup keeps for up to 3 days in the refrigerator or can be frozen in serving-size portions for up to 2 months.

lentils & vegetables

A rich source of vegetable protein, lentils are an excellent food for babies. Ensure they are well cooked and consider including a little garlic and onion.

2 tablespoons lentils or split peas

2 tablespoons mashed mixed vegetables

milk or cooled boiled water

cottage cheese (optional)

Prep time: 5 minutes

Cooking time: 25 minutes

Makes 1 serve

Rinse the lentils or split peas under cold running water and drain. Bring a saucepan of water to the boil, add the lentils or split peas and cook for 20–25 minutes, or until tender.

Drain, then process in a blender or small food processor with the vegetables and a little milk or cooled boiled water to give a smooth consistency. Add a little cottage cheese if desired and mix well.

As baby gets older, simply mash the cooked ingredients together with a fork to produce a lumpier consistency.

chicken, lentils & vegetables

Steam 1 boneless, skinless chicken tenderloin until cooked through. Add to the food processor with the lentils and vegetables and blend until smooth. As baby gets older and is starting to eat lumpier food, finely chop the steamed chicken and mash the cooked lentils and vegetables with a fork until lumpy, rather than pureé them.

spinach & potato mash

Potatoes are not only rich in energy-giving carbohydrates but also in vitamin C. Try using the creamy texture of potato mash in combination with other vegetables.

1 potato, peeled

1 tablespoon finely chopped English spinach

milk or cooled boiled water

Prep time: 5 minutes

Cooking time: 10 minutes

Makes 1 serve

Cook the potato in boiling water for about 10 minutes, or until tender. Put the chopped spinach into a small saucepan with 2 teaspoons water. Cook over low heat for 2 minutes, or until the spinach is wilted. Keep the saucepan tightly covered during cooking, then drain to remove any excess liquid.

Mash the potato and stir in the English spinach, adding a little milk or cooled boiled water if necessary to give a smooth consistency.

variations: Peas or broccoli can be easily substituted for the spinach. Ensure that the peas are well blended as whole peas are a choking risk for very young children.

poached fish with potato & peas

White fish has a soft texture and mild flavour that baby should enjoy. Fish is rich in high-quality protein plus vitamins and minerals such as vitamin D and iodine, which are important for growth and development.

60 g (2¼ oz) piece white fish

milk

I small new potato, cut into cubes

2 teaspoons frozen peas

Prep time: 10 minutes
Cooking time: 5 minutes
Makes I serve

Put the fish in a small saucepan and add enough milk to cover. Simmer, covered, for 3–5 minutes, or until tender.

Meanwhile, add the potato and peas to boiling water and cook until tender. Drain. Mash the potato and peas, adding a little milk from the fish.

Remove any bones from the fish, then flake and serve with the mashed vegetables or mix through the vegetables.

INTRODUCING FISH

Fish is a highly nutritious food rich in vitamins, minerals, good-quality protein and omega-3 fats. Choosing the right types of fish for your baby or toddler is important because their small body size means they are more susceptible to the high mercury levels of some types of fish.

Babies and young children who eat fish regularly should avoid shark (flake), billfish (swordfish/broadbill and marlin) orange roughy (deep sea perch) and catfish. For more information, contact your local food authority.

stewed beef & vegetables

Iron is an important nutrient for babies and toddlers. Meals with iron-rich meats should be on the menu regularly to keep iron stores topped up.

90 g (3¼ oz) lean round or chuck steak or veal steak

1 new potato

1 small carrot

1 baby onion

½ garlic clove, crushed

small piece of bay leaf

sprig of parsley

Prep time: 5 minutes

Cooking time: 40 minutes

Makes 2 serves

Put the steak, potato, carrot and onion in a small saucepan. Add the garlic, the piece of bay leaf and parsley sprig, then cover with water. Cover, bring to the boil, then simmer gently until the meat is tender. Add more water as needed.

Discard the bay leaf and parsley. Blend the ingredients with a little of the cooking liquid.

steamed chicken & apple

The mild flavour of chicken teams well with the sweetness of fruit. Using a fruit that baby is familiar with helps to introduce her to a new flavour.

½ red cooking apple, peeled and cored

2 boneless, skinless chicken tenderloins

Prep time: 10 minutes
Cooking time: 5 minutes
Makes 1 serve

Thinly slice the apple and cut the chicken into small cubes. Place the chicken tenderloin pieces in a steamer and arrange the apple slices over the chicken. Set over a saucepan of boiling water and steam for about 5 minutes, or until tender.

Purée or finely chop the chicken and apple, together with a little of the cooking liquid.

steamed chicken & pumpkin

Cut 100 g (3½ oz) pumpkin (winter squash) into 5 mm (¼ inch) thick slices and steam with the chicken for 5 minutes, or until the pumpkin is tender and the chicken is cooked. Pureé or finely chop the pumpkin and chicken and mix with a little ricotta cheese if desired.

homemade rusks

As your baby discovers her hands she will want to use them to get everything within reach to her mouth. Offering a rusk when this happens will launch your baby into the world of finger food.

1 loaf unsliced wholemeal (whole-wheat) bread

Prep time: 10 minutes
Cooking time: 1 hour
Makes about 80

Preheat the oven to 130°C (250°F/Gas 1). Cut the bread into 2.5 cm (1 inch) thick slices. Remove the crusts and cut each slice into strips about 1.5 cm (½ inch) wide.

Bake the strips on an ungreased baking tray for about 1 hour, or until the rusks are dry and crisp. Turn them occasionally.

Cool and store in an airtight container for up to 7 days.

yeast extract & cheese rusks

Preheat the oven to 150°C (300°F/Gas 2). Spread slices of day-old bread with yeast extract and cover with a thin layer of grated cheddar cheese. Cut into fingers and bake for 1½–2 hours until really hard. Store these rusks in an airtight container.

semolina pudding

The grainy texture of this nourishing pudding helps with the introduction of more textured foods to baby's diet.

2 tablespoons semolina

1 teaspoon unsalted butter

250 ml (9 fl oz/1 cup) milk or cooled boiled water

Prep time: 5 minutes

Cooking time: 5 minutes

Makes 1 serve

Put the semolina in a small saucepan, then add the butter and milk. Simmer, covered, until the semolina is completely tender.

variation: Stir in 1 tablespoon each of finely chopped sultanas (golden raisins) and dried apricots with the butter and milk.

INTRODUCING TEXTURE

While baby's first solids should have a smooth texture, she will soon need variety in the preparation. This will come naturally from the type of fruit, vegetable or cereal you give her – compare the silky smoothness of puréed pumpkin (winter squash) to the grainy feel of puréed broccoli or cauliflower – but you will also need to start to 'process' her foods less.

So, once she is competently managing puréed foods move her along to foods with lumps and bumps in them. Do this by not blending foods for as long, using a fork to mash where you can and allowing her to have a go at finger foods like the rusks on page 45.

from 9 months

AS BABY LEARNS TO EAT:

• *Continue to offer milk. If you are breast-feeding, baby can feed as often as she (and you) like. If baby is bottle-fed, keep feeds to under 800 ml (28 fl oz) a day, as the milk can affect the quantity of other food baby eats.*

• *Chop rather than mash food, even if baby has no teeth.*

• *Watch out for hard foods. Babies can easily gag or choke.*

• *Teach your baby to wash her hands before and after eating.*

• *Always be on hand, since babies can have trouble with the softest of foods.*

This stage can start at anywhere from 8 to 9 months. Once baby is eating three times a day you may have difficulty thinking of what to feed her at times. By now baby may already be eating little snacks or finger foods. Some babies are determined to feed themselves; others are content to sit back and let you do it most of the time. It is worth encouraging the reluctant finger food eater, as it gives you a bit of time off to eat your own meal when you are eating together.

By the time your child reaches her first birthday she will be eating many foods that the family normally eats. She needs a healthy variety of foods and will be able to chew many of them, though it is still important to avoid hard foods, such as raw vegetables.

choking

Babies learn by putting things into their mouths. They will put anything that fits into their mouths, from burst balloons to tiny batteries — and consequently choking is a major hazard for the under-twos. We want them to put food in their mouths, but pieces of hard food are potential choking hazards, which is why experts advise against giving babies and toddlers certain foods (refer to the 'hard foods' chart on page 17 for specific examples).

Don't let the thought of your baby choking put you off giving her finger foods and other foods such as apples and carrot. Your baby will learn to eat these foods, but in the process may gag. A baby can gag on any food while she is learning to swallow and chew. In fact, babies have a gagging reflex which activates when they swallow too much, whether it is soft or hard.

When baby has teeth she may bite off a piece that is too large and because she is still learning to chew she may try to swallow it. This can cause gagging, but mostly baby will cough it up. If not you can hook the food out with your finger. Because this can happen it is important that baby is never left to eat alone.

While baby is learning to chew you can give her soft finger foods and cut up other foods or grate foods like carrot and apple.

simple scrambled eggs

Eggs are a good source of protein and fat plus valuable vitamins and minerals. In fact, they contain every nutrient except vitamin C, making them an important part of a growing baby's diet.

I whole egg
I egg yolk
I tablespoon milk
I teaspoon unsalted butter

Prep time: 2 minutes
Cooking time: 4 minutes
Makes I serve

Lightly beat together the whole egg and egg yolk with the milk. Melt the butter in a small non-stick frying pan over low heat and pour in the egg mixture. Cook, stirring occasionally, until the egg begins to set underneath. This will take about 3–4 minutes. Stir lightly and cook until just set. Serve the scrambled eggs with lightly toasted bread.

variations: Try adding grated cheese and chopped cooked chicken for a more substantial meal. Alternatively, fold through finely chopped wilted baby English spinach leaves and finely chopped tomatoes.

INTRODUCING EGGS

Allergy to egg is the most common food allergy among children. Fortunately, most children grow out of it by the time they go to school. Egg white is the most likely offender in egg allergy and this is the reason why the yolk rather than the whole egg is introduced to babies first, at around 8–9 months. If all goes well with this, then the white or whole egg can be introduced at around 10 months. When introducing either part of the egg make sure it is well cooked — allergy-causing proteins in food can cause a stronger reaction if they are not cooked.

carrot & pumpkin risotto

This recipe uses vegetables your baby knows and is her start on family foods. Blend it in the beginning stages of baby's feeding development if necessary.

90 g (3¼ oz) unsalted butter

1 onion, finely chopped

250 g (9 oz) pumpkin (winter squash), cut into small cubes

2 carrots, cut into small cubes

1.75–2 litres (61–70 fl oz/ 7–8 cups) salt-reduced vegetable stock

440 g (15½ oz/2 cups) risotto rice

90 g (3¼ oz/1 cup) freshly grated parmesan cheese

¼ teaspoon ground nutmeg

Prep time: 15 minutes

Cooking time: 35 minutes

Makes 4 serves

Heat 60 g (2¼ oz) of the butter in a large, heavy-based saucepan. Add the onion and fry for 1–2 minutes, or until soft. Add the pumpkin and carrot and cook for 6–8 minutes, or until tender. Mash slightly with a potato masher. Put the stock in a separate saucepan and keep at simmering point.

Add the rice to the vegetables and cook for 1 minute, stirring constantly. Ladle in enough hot stock to cover the rice; stir well. Reduce the heat and add more stock as it is absorbed, stirring frequently. Continue until the rice is tender and creamy (this will take about 25 minutes).

Remove the pan from the heat, add the remaining butter, cheese and nutmeg and season with freshly ground black pepper. Fork through. Cover and leave for 5 minutes before serving.

HINT: Left-over risotto is great the next day formed into balls and deep-fried. Ensure the balls are cool before serving them to baby.

cheesy stars

Pasta is a great quick-cook food for kids of all ages and with more than six-hundred named shapes of pasta, this meal need never be the same!

60 g (2¼ oz/⅔ cup) small, star-shaped pasta (see hint)

1 teaspoon unsalted butter

1 tablespoon grated cheese

1 tablespoon milk

chopped parsley

Prep time: 5 minutes
Cooking time: 10 minutes
Makes 1 serve

Cook the pasta in boiling water for about 8–9 minutes, or until tender.

Drain, return the pasta to the saucepan, then add the butter, cheese and milk. Mix well and stir over low heat for 1 minute, or until the butter and cheese have melted. Stir in a little parsley. If necessary, mash to serve.

variation: You could substitute the star-shaped pasta for any number of other small pasta shapes. Use larger spirals and bow-shaped pasta for babies as they show more interest in finger foods.

HINT: Small star-shaped pasta is about the size of a split pea.

steamed fish & diced vegetables

It's not just babies that need to eat fish, health authorities recommend we all have at least one or two fish meals a week.

60 g (2¼ oz) piece boneless white fish, cut into cubes

2 tablespoons finely diced vegetables (asparagus, broccoli, carrot, frozen peas)

milk (optional)

Prep time: 10 minutes

Cooking time: 8 minutes

Makes 1 serve

Put the fish with the vegetables in a steamer and set over a saucepan of boiling water. Steam for about 8 minutes, or until tender.

Mash the fish and vegetables together to form a smooth consistency, adding a little of the cooking liquid or milk if necessary. Otherwise, flake the fish and chop the accompanying vegetables, adding a little milk or cooking liquid.

cauliflower in creamy sauce

When well cooked, this dish makes a creamy meal for younger babies. With less cooking, the firm florets makes an ideal finger food for the older baby.

60 g (2¼ oz) fresh or frozen cauliflower, cut into small florets

2 tablespoons milk

1 teaspoon dry milk powder or ricotta cheese

¾ teaspoon cornflour (cornstarch)

Prep time: 5 minutes

Cooking time: 8 minutes

Makes 1 serve

Cut the cauliflower into small florets and boil or steam until tender. Drain well.

Put the milk, milk powder or ricotta cheese and cornflour in a small saucepan. Cook, stirring, until thickened.

Finely chop or mash the cauliflower and stir into the sauce.

HINT: This recipe can also be used for diced carrots, tiny florets of broccoli, diced asparagus or pumpkin (winter squash).

dal

Lentils are a powerhouse of nutrition. Excellent as a source of protein, iron and zinc, they provide a valuable alternative to meat.

310 g (11 oz/1¼ cups) red lentils

30 g (1 oz) unsalted butter

1 medium onion, finely chopped

2 garlic cloves, crushed

1 teaspoon grated fresh ginger

1 teaspoon ground turmeric

1 teaspoon garam masala

Prep time: 15 minutes

Cooking time: 20 minutes

Makes 4–6 serves

Put the lentils in a large bowl and cover with water. Remove any floating particles and drain the lentils well.

Heat the butter in a saucepan. Fry the onion for about 3 minutes, or until soft. Add the garlic, ginger and spices; cook, stirring for another minute.

Add the lentils and 500 ml (17 fl oz/2 cups) water and bring to the boil. Lower the heat and simmer, stirring occasionally, for 15 minutes, or until all the water has been absorbed. Watch carefully towards the end of cooking time, as the mixture could burn on the bottom of the pan.

Transfer to a serving bowl and serve warm or at room temperature with pitta toasts or with naan or pitta bread.

pitta toasts

Preheat the oven to 180°C (350°F/Gas 4). Cut 4 rounds of pitta bread into wedges and brush lightly with oil. Arrange on a baking tray and cook for 5–7 minutes, or until lightly browned and crisp.

lamb shank & barley casserole

Rich with flavour, this dish is well worth the time. It is also big on protein, the minerals iron and zinc and soluble barley fibre (the gentle type).

1 tablespoon olive oil

1 small onion, finely chopped

1 garlic clove, crushed (optional)

50 g (1¾ oz/⅓ cup) diced carrot

2 tablespoons finely diced celery

2 teaspoons finely chopped rosemary

2 French trimmed lamb shanks (about 600 g/1 lb 5 oz)

plain (all-purpose) flour, for dusting

2 tablespoons pearl barley

500 ml (17 fl oz/2 cups) salt-reduced beef stock

Prep time: 15 minutes

Cooking time: 2 hours 10 minutes

Makes 3—4 serves

Heat the oil in a small flameproof casserole dish or heavy-based saucepan. Add the onion, garlic, carrot, celery and rosemary and cook over medium heat for about 5 minutes, or until soft.

Dust the lamb shanks in flour, shaking off any excess. Add to the dish, turning to brown all sides. Add the barley and stock and bring to the boil. Reduce the heat to low and cook, covered, for 2 hours, or until the meat is very tender and falling away from the bone.

Remove the shanks, allow to cool slightly, then remove the meat from the bone, discarding any sinew. Cut the meat into small pieces and return to the casserole, stirring to combine. For a smoother texture put in a food processor and lightly process. This meal can be frozen for up to 3 months. Thaw, then reheat to serve.

vegetable casserole

The foundations of healthy eating are now laid. By making vegetables a regular part of baby's menu, you will guarantee they are enjoyed in the future.

1 tablespoon olive oil

½ onion, finely chopped

1 garlic clove, crushed (optional)

½ celery stalk, finely diced

½ carrot, diced

50 g (1¾ oz/¼ cup) brown lentils

200 g (7 oz) tinned diced tomatoes

185 ml (6 fl oz/¾ cup) salt-reduced vegetable or chicken stock

150 g (5½ oz) pumpkin (winter squash), deseeded and cut into 1 cm (½ inch) cubes

½ zucchini (courgette), quartered lengthways and cut into 1 cm (½ inch) slices

Prep time: 15 minutes

Cooking time: 1 hour

Makes 3–4 serves

Preheat the oven to 200°C (400°F/Gas 6).

Heat the oil in a flameproof casserole dish over medium heat. Add the onion, garlic, celery and carrot and cook for 5 minutes, or until softened. Add the lentils, tomato and stock and stir to combine. Cover and bake for 40 minutes. Add the pumpkin and zucchini and cook for a further 10–12 minutes, or until tender.

Mash lightly with a fork to serve if necessary.

rice pudding

Good rice pudding takes time — make this recipe as a special dessert for the whole family. Add some sultanas (golden raisins) to boost its fibre and sweetness.

110 g (3¾ oz/½ cup) risotto rice

1 litre (35 fl oz/4 cups) milk

2 tablespoons caster (superfine) sugar

1 teaspoon natural vanilla extract

1 teaspoon unsalted butter (optional)

pinch of cinnamon (optional)

fresh berries, to garnish (optional)

Prep time: 10 minutes
Cooking time: 1½ hours
Makes 4 serves

Preheat the oven to 180°C (350°F/Gas 4).

Place the rice, milk, sugar, vanilla and butter and cinnamon, if using, in a baking dish and stir.

Bake for about 1½ hours, stirring every 15 minutes to make sure it doesn't stick to the dish. Remove the pudding from the oven when it has the consistency of creamed rice. Do not overcook or it may dry out. Cool slightly and top with fresh berries.

fresh fruit salad

Soft chunks of ripe seasonal fruit make baby's first fruit salad a delightful exploration of taste and texture. For younger babies, simply mash the fruits.

100 g (3½ oz) seedless watermelon, cut into 2 cm (¾ inch) cubes

100 g (3½ oz) orange-fleshed melon, cut into 2 cm (¾ inch) cubes

60 g (2¼ oz) strawberries, hulled and cut into quarters

½ kiwi fruit, peeled and cut into pieces

50 g (1¾ oz) seedless white grapes, halved

¼ banana, sliced

1–2 tablespoons unsweetened fruit juice or orange juice

Prep time: 5 minutes

Cooking time: Nil

Makes 2–3 serves

Place the fruits in a bowl, pour over the orange juice and toss to coat. Serve as finger food or cut up into smaller pieces for spoon feeding.

HINT: You can substitute any seasonal fruits for the above suggestions. Avoid fruits with seeds, though, unless you can remove them first.

fruit jelly

Jelly (gelatine dessert) is a tasty textural delight for toddlers. This recipe is also a vitamin- and fibre-packed alternative to ready-made varieties.

1 tablespoon gelatine powder

375 ml (13 fl oz/1½ cups) unsweetened fruit juice

200 g (7 oz/¾ cup) puréed fresh or drained, tinned fruit in natural juice

Prep time: 10 minutes

Cooking time: 5 minutes

Makes 6 serves

Sprinkle the gelatine over 125 ml (4 fl oz/½ cup) cool water in a small saucepan. Heat through, then add the fruit juice and heat through again. Pour into a mixing bowl and leave until it begins to thicken. Stir in the puréed fruit until well combined.

Transfer to small dishes and refrigerate until set.

yoghurt jelly

This is a good source of vitamin C plus the important minerals calcium and phosphorus. Use a Greek-style yoghurt for an extra creamy version.

1½ tablespoons gelatine powder

375 ml (13 fl oz/1½ cups) unsweetened fruit juice

250 g (9 oz/1 cup) plain yoghurt

Prep time: 10 minutes

Cooking time: 5 minutes

Makes 6 serves

Sprinkle the gelatine over 125 ml (4 fl oz/½ cup) cool water in a small saucepan. Heat through, then add the fruit juice and heat through again. Pour into a mixing bowl and leave until it begins to thicken. Stir in the yoghurt, then beat with electric beaters until fluffy.

Transfer to small dishes and refrigerate until set.

Independence is a feature of toddlers' behaviour and meal times are a perfect time to show it. Appetites will wane and fads and fussiness will come and go. Stay relaxed with food and your toddler will too. Cleaning up a plate is not what it is all about. Instead, trust your toddler to tell you when they are full. Make sure the food they get is good and healthy *most* of the time.

toddler food

1 year & on

By the time your child reaches his first birthday he will have tried a wide range of foods and you will be able to include him in many of the meals you make for yourself or the rest of the family.

During their second year children start to assert their independence and parents can become frustrated when they find their child being finicky about food. Toddlers can clamp their mouths shut or tip their food on the floor, just to get your attention.

tricks for trouble-free meal times

If you find that your toddler is being stubborn at meal times there are strategies you can employ to help avoid meals turning into battles. If you have a child who is taking a stand over meal times be assured that you are not alone. By offering him a wide range of wholesome foods he will not starve. It will also help if you follow these suggestions:

• Try to eat as a family as often as you can. This may only be possible at the weekends, or only at breakfast time, but it is important. When your toddler sees you eating something he will want to copy. At this age children are natural copycats and this is an easy way to educate children about food and table manners. Children who eat alone often develop bad habits. If you can't eat together then at least sit with your child, put his chair up to the table and make it a special time. You need to to be there to supervise.

Plonking your child down in front of the television set with a bowl of finger food or a favourite meal may seem like an easy way out. However, in the long run it is not adding to your toddler's enjoyment of food or meal times and it may actually lead to fussy eating. Television can also be a problem if the program includes advertisements for junk foods or food that is high in fat, sugar or salt.

• Feed your child the same foods that you normally eat. If you taste commercial baby or toddler food you will be amazed at its blandness — and its sameness. Some home-made dishes will need to be presented to your toddler over and over again before he eats them — and a few he may never eat. But if he sees you eating the same food he may decide he is missing out on something and try it himself.

• Keep challenging his food horizons. Continue to present him with new variations on the food he is eating. If you eat the same foods every night of the week, and so does he, he will never learn about new foods. If you are eating a Thai meal or a curry try him out with a little bit of mild food. Some children take to lightly spiced food more quickly than others.

• Give him the freshest, most nutritious and best-quality food that you can buy and make.

• Set a good example. If you don't eat fruit and vegetables you can't expect your child to want them. If you haven't been in the habit of eating four or five vegetables and two or three pieces of fruit a day, then start today.

• Avoid food battles. If your child refuses to eat something one day offer it again another day — and another day again. Don't get into an argument.

• Cheat. You can hide vegetables in meat sauces, meatballs or casseroles. You can hide milk in sauces, custards or ice cream. Be creative. You can serve fish and chips (fries) on paper towels or in a clean takeaway food box, or wrap up a burger. You can use a pastry cutter to make cheese into star shapes or turn a salad into a face by cutting a cheese circle, popping on a cherry tomato nose, two sultana (golden raisin) eyes, a cucumber mouth and lettuce hair! You can make iceblocks (popsicles/ice lollies) out of frozen bananas on a stick, or milkshakes from milk blended with fruit.

• Let him help get the meal ready. There are many simple things toddlers can do — fetch and carry anything unbreakable, wash vegetables or fruit, stir simple mixes and shake dressings.

• Feed him at around the same times each day. Toddlers are creatures of habit so they like a routine.

• If he is having a bad day and you feel he won't eat anything, put together a plate with a choice of foods, such as dried apricots, cooked chicken, cooked pasta, a slice of banana, a cube of cheese, a couple of stoned olives or cherry tomatoes, two or three cooked beans or snow peas (mangetout), or a piece of wholemeal (whole-wheat) bread with his favourite spread.

• Don't reward with desserts or sweets (candy) to make your child eat a particular food he doesn't like. This can actually make children dislike the food in question even more. Bribing your child with sweets only raises their importance in his eyes. Only give him dessert if he is still hungry after he has eaten his other food. Children are more likely to want a food when they are told they can't have it or if it is used as a reward. That said, it is important to allow treats sometimes.

It won't hurt your child if he refuses the occasional meal. Nagging, cajoling or shouting is not going to help.

breakfast

Your toddler needs breakfast, just as you do. Skipping breakfast has been found to be behind poor concentration and forgetfulness — and this applies to children as well as adults. After hours of fasting while you were asleep, your brain needs fuel in order to function properly. If your toddler sees you skipping breakfast he will want to copy you — and that is not good for either of you.

Research has also found that children who eat breakfast have better overall diets than those who skip this meal. They are also more likely to achieve the recommended daily amounts of vitamins and minerals than those who don't eat breakfast.

Breakfast is a good time to consume a range of nutrients including fibre in cereal and bread; protein and calcium in milk and yoghurt; and vitamins, minerals and fibre in fruit.

It is important to give yourself enough time for breakfast as well as getting lunches and snacks ready if you have to take them to childcare. Being prepared the night before is always a good start. You can pack some of the snacks, put lunchboxes out, get out cereal bowls, cereal and cutlery and have the kitchen ready.

breakfast on the go

Mornings can be a challenge when everyone has to be ready on time. Consider these quick breakfast suggestions:

- Home-made muesli (granola) with yoghurt and fruit
- Quick-cook microwave oats (porridge)
- Fresh fruit salad with yoghurt
- Baked beans and toast fingers
- Fruit toast spread with ricotta or cream cheese
- Fruit and yoghurt smoothies
- Omelettes or scrambled eggs

home-made muesli

While adult commercial cereals can be used for a toddler's breakfast, some are high in sugar and salt. This muesli (granola) has all the goodness of whole grains and dried fruits without any unwanted extras.

150 g (5½ oz/1½ cups) rolled (porridge) oats

2 tablespoons wheatgerm

30 g (1 oz/¼ cup) raw oatmeal

20 g (¾ oz/¼ cup) bran

60 g (2¼ oz/½ cup) sultanas (golden raisins)

30 g (1 oz/⅓ cup) dried apple, chopped

90 g (3¼ oz/½ cup) dried apricots, chopped

Prep time: 10 minutes

Cooking time: Nil

Serves 8

Combine all the ingredients together and store in an airtight container for up to 4 weeks. To serve, pour over a little milk, place in a saucepan and stir over medium heat for 30–60 seconds to soften; or place in a microwave for 20–30 seconds.

Alternatively, blend the dry muesli in a food processor until almost fine. Serve with other dried fruits, fresh fruit, yoghurt or a drizzle of honey (only for children over 12 months) or fruit purée.

banana porridge

A wholegrain cereal like oats is rich in energy-giving carbohydrates, essential fats and minerals. Team it with banana and it becomes a great source of B vitamins including folate, as well as vitamin C and potassium.

1 tablespoon quick-cook oats

1 tablespoon cold water

1½ tablespoons hot water

2 teaspoons mashed banana

milk or cooled boiled water

Prep time: 5 minutes

Cooking time: 2 minutes

Serves 1

Combine the quick-cook oats with the cold water in a small saucepan. Add the hot water and bring to the boil, stirring. Reduce the heat and simmer for 30 seconds or until the mixture is thick and creamy.

Remove the porridge from the heat and stir through the mashed banana. Mix with enough milk or cooled boiled water to produce the required consistency.

fluffy omelette

The ultimate in convenience food, eggs make a perfect meal at any time of the day for a growing toddler — don't just save them for breakfast!

I egg yolk
2 egg whites
I teaspoon unsalted butter

Prep time: 5 minutes
Cooking time: 5 minutes
Serves I

Lightly beat the egg yolk with I teaspoon water. Beat the egg whites to soft peaks and stir in the yolk mixture.

Melt the butter in a small frying pan and pour in the egg mixture. Cook quickly on one side, then turn and cook until just firm.

variations: Fillings of flaked fish such as red salmon, finely chopped sautéed zucchini (courgette) and onion, mushrooms, tomato or grated cheddar cheese can be used. Place along the centre of the omelette on the uncooked side, then fold over to enclose the filling. Cook until the omelette is cooked through, turning once.

eggs en cocotte

Research shows that a healthy diet is encouraged when children eat with their family regularly. Enjoy this recipe with your toddler as a special breakfast.

TOMATO SAUCE

1 tablespoon olive oil

1 garlic clove, crushed

3 vine-ripened tomatoes (about 300 g/10½ oz), peeled, seeded and chopped

½ teaspoon olive oil

4 eggs

2 tablespoons snipped chives

4 slices thick wholegrain bread

15 g (½ oz) unsalted butter

Prep time: 15 minutes

Cooking time: 30 minutes

Serves 4

Preheat the oven to 180°C (350°F/Gas 4). To make the tomato sauce, heat the oil in a heavy-based frying pan. Add the garlic and cook for 30 seconds. Add the tomato and season with salt and freshly ground black pepper. Cook over medium heat for 15 minutes, or until thickened.

Grease four 125 ml (4 fl oz/½ cup) ramekins with the olive oil, then carefully break 1 egg into each, trying not to break the yolk. Pour the tomato sauce evenly around the outside of each egg, so the yolk is still visible. Sprinkle with chives and season lightly with salt and freshly ground black pepper.

Place the ramekins in a deep baking dish and pour in enough hot water to come halfway up the outside of the ramekins. Bake for about 10–12 minutes, or until the egg white is set. Toast the bread and lightly spread the slices with the butter, then cut into thick fingers. Serve immediately with the cooked eggs.

french toast

Bread is an important staple food for the growing toddler. Vary the types of bread you use for this recipe by using wholegrain, rye or even fruit bread.

I egg, lightly beaten

2 teaspoons milk

2 thick slices wholemeal (whole-wheat) bread

unsalted butter or oil, for frying

pinch of cinnamon (optional)

Prep time: 5 minutes

Cooking time: 2 minutes

Serves 2

Beat the egg with the milk. Cut two slices of the wholemeal bread into different shapes, using shaped biscuit (cookie) cutters. Dip the bread into the egg mixture. Cook in a non-stick frying pan, brushed with a little melted butter or oil, until golden on both sides. Sprinkle with a little cinnamon, if desired.

cat toast

Cut the bread into the shape of a cat face by trimming away the lower corners of the slice to make a rounded chin and cheeks. Shape the top edge into a rounded head with two pointed ears. Dip into the egg mixture and fry in butter to make french toast, then add halved dried apricots for eyes, a raisin for the nose and a thin strip of orange zest for the mouth.

scrambled eggs with sweet corn sauce

The combination of eggs, with their high-quality protein, and corn, rich in carbohydrate, makes this meal a great start to the day for energetic toddlers.

250 g (9 oz/1 cup) tinned creamed corn

15 g (½ oz) unsalted butter

2½ teaspoons cornflour (cornstarch)

250 ml (9 fl oz/1 cup) milk

6 eggs

1 tablespoon milk, extra

1–2 teaspoons unsalted butter, extra

Prep time: 10 minutes
Cooking time: 10 minutes
Serves 4

Put the corn and butter in a saucepan. Combine the cornflour and 1 tablespoon of the milk in a bowl, then add the remaining milk, stirring well. Pour into the saucepan and bring to the boil. Simmer, stirring, for 2–3 minutes, until the sauce thickens. Keep warm.

Beat the eggs and extra milk together and season with freshly ground black pepper. Melt the extra butter in a frying pan and pour in the egg mixture. Cook gently, stirring occasionally, for 2–3 minutes, or until just firm. Transfer to a plate and pour on the sweet corn sauce.

home-made baked beans

Soya beans are the perfect size for tiny fingers to practise their fine motor skills. They also provide vitamins, high-quality protein, iron and zinc.

550 g (1 lb 4 oz/3 cups) dried soya beans

400 g (14 oz/1⅔ cups) tinned diced tomatoes

250 ml (9 fl oz/1 cup) salt-reduced vegetable stock

1 bay leaf

2 tablespoons chopped parsley

pinch of dried thyme

1 tablespoon vegetable oil

Prep time: 5 minutes
Cooking time: 4 hours 40 minutes
Serves 4

Cook the soya beans in plenty of water for about 4 hours, or until tender. Drain. Preheat the oven to 180°C (350°F/Gas 4).

Put the soya beans in a casserole dish and add the tomato, stock, herbs and oil. Bake, covered, for 40 minutes.

HINTS: If you want a thicker consistency, remove the lid of the casserole dish and cook for a further 10–15 minutes, or until reduced to the desired consistency. Instead of using dried soya beans, you can use the same amount of drained tinned soya beans.

blueberry pancakes

A source of vitamins A, C and the B group, blueberries make these pancakes a much healthier breakfast for toddlers than pancakes with maple syrup.

250 g (9 oz/2 cups) plain (all-purpose) flour

2 teaspoons baking powder

1 teaspoon bicarbonate of soda (baking soda)

90 g (3¼ oz/⅓ cup) sugar

2 eggs

80 g (2¾ oz) unsalted butter, melted

310 ml (10¾ fl oz/1¼ cups) milk

310 g (11 oz/2 cups) blueberries, fresh or frozen

Prep time: 10–15 minutes
Cooking time: 18 minutes
Makes 6

Sift the flour, baking powder and bicarbonate of soda into a large bowl. Add the sugar and make a well in the centre. Using a fork, whisk the eggs, melted butter and milk together in a bowl and add to the dry ingredients, stirring just to combine (add more milk if you prefer a thinner batter). Gently fold in the blueberries.

Heat a frying pan and brush lightly with melted butter or oil. Pour 125 ml (4 fl oz/½ cup) batter into the pan and spread out to make a pancake about 15 cm (6 inches) in diameter. Cook over low heat until bubbles appear and pop on the surface.

Turn the pancake over and cook the other side (these pancakes can be difficult to handle so take care when turning). Transfer to a plate and cover with a tea towel (dish towel) to keep warm while cooking the remaining batter. The pancakes are delicious served warm with blueberry coulis (see recipe below) and Greek-style plain yoghurt.

HINT: If you use frozen blueberries there is no need to thaw them.

blueberry coulis

Put 310 g (11 oz/2 cups) fresh or frozen blueberries in a blender or food processor and blend until pureéd. Strain through a fine sieve to remove the skin and to make a smooth sauce. Stir in 2 teaspoons icing (confectioners') sugar. Stir the coulis through plain yoghurt or serve plain with pancakes, ice cream, fruit salad or breakfast cereal. Store any left-over coulis in the refrigerator for up to 3 days. Makes 150 ml (5 fl oz).

mushrooms with toast fingers

Mushrooms are as rich in the B vitamin niacin as red meat. They provide a flavoursome breakfast that can be enjoyed by the whole family.

MUSHROOM SAUCE

1 tablespoon olive oil

800 g (1 lb 12 oz/8 cups) mixed mushrooms (flat, button, open-cap), chopped

2 garlic cloves, crushed

1 teaspoon finely chopped thyme

125 ml (4 fl oz/½ cup) salt-reduced vegetable stock

1 large handful parsley, finely chopped

4 slices thick wholemeal (whole-wheat) bread

baby English spinach (optional)

shaved parmesan cheese (optional)

Prep time: 10 minutes

Cooking time: 20 minutes

Serves 4

Heat the olive oil in a large frying pan. Add the mixed mushrooms and cook over high heat for 4–5 minutes, or until soft. Add the garlic and thyme. Season and cook for 2–3 minutes. Add 185 ml (6 fl oz/¾ cup) water. Cook until it has evaporated. Add the stock, then reduce the heat. Cook for a further 3–4 minutes, or until the stock has reduced and thickened. Add the parsley.

Grill (broil) or toast the bread until golden on both sides. Slice into fingers, if desired. Divide among the serving plates and top with the mushrooms. Top with baby English spinach leaves and parmesan shavings, if desired.

dried fruit compote with yoghurt

This fruity breakfast is full of flavour and is a great source of fibre, calcium and potassium with small but important amounts of iron and beta-carotene.

50 g (1¾ oz/⅓ cup) dried apricots, quartered

50 g (1¾ oz/¼ cup) stoned prunes, quartered

50 g (1¾ oz/⅔ cup) dried pears, chopped

50 g (1¾ oz/⅔ cup) dried peaches, chopped

185 ml (6 fl oz/¾ cup) orange juice

1 cinnamon stick

plain yoghurt, to serve

Prep time: 5 minutes
Cooking time: 10 minutes
Serves 4

Put the fruit, orange juice and cinnamon stick in a saucepan and stir to combine. Bring to the boil, then reduce the heat to low, cover, and simmer for 10 minutes, or until the fruit is plump and softened. Discard the cinnamon stick. Serve drizzled with the cooking liquid and a dollop of the plain yoghurt.

Store in an airtight container in the refrigerator for up to 1 week.

mixed berry couscous

Fruit-based breakfasts are rich in vitamins, minerals and fibre, and are a quick and yummy way for kids to start the day. If berries aren't in season use a medley of whatever happens to be ripe and tasty in your fruit bowl.

185 g (6½ oz/1 cup) instant couscous

500 ml (17 fl oz/2 cups) apple and cranberry juice

1 cinnamon stick

250 g (9 oz/2 cups) frozen raspberries, thawed

250 g (9 oz/1⅔ cups) frozen blueberries, thawed

2 teaspoons orange zest, plus extra, to garnish

250 g (9 oz/1⅔ cups) strawberries, halved

185 g (6½ oz/¾ cup) Greek-style plain yoghurt

fresh mint leaves, to garnish

Prep time: 15 minutes
Cooking time: 5 minutes
Serves 4

Put the instant couscous in a bowl. Pour the apple and cranberry juice into a saucepan and add the cinnamon stick. Cover and bring to the boil, then remove from the heat and pour over the couscous. Cover the couscous with plastic wrap and leave for about 5 minutes, or until all the liquid has been absorbed. After this time, remove the cinnamon stick from the bowl.

Gently pat the thawed berries with paper towels to absorb the excess juices. Separate the grains of couscous with a fork, then gently fold in the orange zest and most of the berries. Spoon the couscous mixture into four serving bowls and sprinkle with the remaining berries. Serve with a generous dollop of the yoghurt. Garnish with mint leaves and orange zest and serve.

lunch

The type of lunch your child has will depend on whether he is at home with you, out with you or at childcare, preschool or kindergarten. If he is in childcare it will depend on whether he needs to take his own lunch or whether the centre prepares the midday meal.

If you are packing the lunch, you will know what he has had for breakfast and will be able to prepare different types of food for lunch. If your child is served lunch at childcare check the menu to be sure that you don't give your child the same type of food for dinner as he had at lunchtime.

One of the most fun lunches to have with a toddler is a picnic. You can pack a picnic and take it with you to your own backyard, the nearest park, to a bench while you are out shopping or to the beach. It can be an opportunity to get together with other parents or just to get out. Remember that if it is a warm or hot day the safest way to travel with food, even sandwiches, is for it to be in an insulated bag.

lunch in a hurry

When kids are hungry they often need food immediately. Consider these suggestions for a quick solution to a fast lunch:

• Microwave or bake a potato, cut it in half and serve it topped with a tin of baked beans or creamed corn.

• Keep left-over pasta in the refrigerator to team with a tin of tuna or salmon plus any combination of the following: quartered cherry tomatoes, cooked frozen peas, tinned sweet corn, grated cheese or avocado.

• Mash up some avocado with cream cheese and serve with toast fingers for dipping.

• Scrambled eggs or omelettes — don't just reserve these for breakfast.

• Cheese and ham or tomato on toast.

chicken meatballs in soup

Be it laziness or just tired little jaws, toddlers often don't manage meat well. Meat needs to be presented in a way toddlers can manage (without puréeing). Minced (ground) meat, as in this recipe, is the perfect solution.

1 spring onion (scallion)

375 g (13 oz) minced (ground) chicken

875 ml (30 fl oz/3½ cups) salt-reduced chicken stock

1½ tablespoons frozen peas

1½ tablespoons finely diced carrot

1 tablespoon alphabet noodles or other small pasta

Prep time: 20 minutes
Cooking time: 20 minutes
Serves 4

Finely chop half the spring onion and thinly slice the remainder. Combine the chicken and finely chopped spring onion until thoroughly mixed, then form into small balls, about the size of walnuts. Bring the chicken stock to the boil in a saucepan and add the peas, carrot and noodles. Simmer until the vegetables are tender, then add the reserved sliced spring onion.

Drop the chicken balls into the simmering soup. Cook until the meatballs float to the surface and turn white.

variation: You can substitute the chicken with the same amount of boneless, skinless chicken breast. Simply cut the chicken into thin slices, place it between two sheets of baking paper and gently pound with a rolling pin to make almost transparent slices. These will cook in seconds in the hot soup.

tomato soup

Soup is a great way to get vegetables into toddlers. Make sure it is cool enough to eat and then let them dunk toast fingers for a nourishing 'hands on' meal.

20 g (¾ oz) unsalted butter

1 celery stalk, finely chopped

1 onion, finely chopped

1 carrot, finely chopped

1 garlic clove, crushed

700 g (1 lb 9 oz/2¾ cups) tomato-based pasta sauce

750 ml (26 fl oz/3 cups) salt-reduced chicken or vegetable stock

1 teaspoon sugar

1 parsley sprig

1 bay leaf

250 ml (9 fl oz/1 cup) milk

2 teaspoons chopped parsley

toast, to serve

Prep time: 10 minutes

Cooking time: 20 minutes

Serves 4

Melt the butter in a saucepan and sauté the celery, onion and carrot for 3–4 minutes. Add the garlic and cook for 30 seconds. Add the pasta sauce, chicken or vegetable stock, sugar, parsley sprig and bay leaf. Bring to the boil, then simmer for 10 minutes. Remove the parsley and bay leaf.

Purée the soup in a blender, then return it to the pan. Stir through the milk and heat until hot.

Garnish with the parsley and serve with toast.

salmon & basil fish cakes

These tasty cakes make a great meal or even a nutritious snack served cold. They are packed with energy-giving carbohydrate, as well as vitamins, minerals (especially calcium if you mash in the salmon bones) and important fats.

2 medium all-purpose potatoes, quartered

415 g (14¾ oz) tinned pink salmon, drained, skin and large bones removed

½ teaspoon grated lime zest

4 spring onions (scallions), finely chopped

1 handful basil leaves, roughly chopped

1 tablespoon capers, rinsed, drained and roughly chopped

1 egg yolk

1 egg, lightly beaten

1 tablespoon milk

40 g (1½ oz/⅓ cup) plain (all-purpose) flour

70 g (2½ oz/¾ cup) dry breadcrumbs

oil, for shallow-frying

Prep time: 20 minutes + 30 minutes refrigeration

Cooking time: 20 minutes

Makes 8

Cook the potatoes in a large saucepan of boiling water until just tender. Drain and lightly mash, leaving some large pieces. Allow the potatoes to cool.

Meanwhile, in a bowl, gently flake the salmon into large pieces. Add the lime zest, spring onion, basil, capers and egg yolk. Mix lightly then stir in the mashed potato. Season with freshly ground black pepper.

Combine the egg and milk in a shallow bowl. Spread the flour and breadcrumbs out on separate plates. With wet hands, shape the salmon mixture into eight patties about 6 cm (2½ inches) in diameter, pressing the mixture firmly together. Dust with flour, and shake off any excess. Dip the fish cakes into the egg mixture, then coat in the breadcrumbs. Place the patties on a tray and refrigerate, covered, for 30 minutes, or until firm.

Add enough oil to come one-third of the way up a large, deep frying pan. Heat over high heat. Cook the patties for 3–4 minutes each side, or until golden and heated through. Drain on paper towels. Serve with mashed sweet potato and minted peas.

HINTS: The patties can be made several hours ahead and refrigerated. You can substitute tinned tuna for salmon if desired.

macaroni cheese

This creamy, cheesy pasta meal always seems to be a firm favourite with toddlers. And the dairy it contains is good for young children, being rich in calcium needed for growing teeth and bones.

30 g (1 oz) unsalted butter

1 tablespoon plain (all-purpose) flour

250 ml (9 fl oz/1 cup) milk

60 g (2¼ oz/½ cup) grated cheese

350 g (12 oz/2¼ cups) macaroni, cooked

1 tomato, cut into wedges

Prep time: 5 minutes
Cooking time: 10 minutes
Serves 4

Melt the butter in a small saucepan. Blend in the flour and cook for 1 minute.

Remove the pan from the heat and gradually blend in the milk. Return to the heat and cook, stirring, until the sauce boils and thickens.

Reduce the heat and simmer for 3 minutes. Add the grated cheese and stir until melted. Mix the macaroni through the sauce and season with freshly ground black pepper to taste. Serve with the tomato wedges.

mini drumsticks

Toddlers enjoy managing their own food at meal times. This recipe will certainly let them do that — just remind them to eat the chicken and not only the sauce!

12 chicken wings, tips removed

cornflour (cornstarch), for dusting

2 egg whites, lightly beaten

175 g (6 oz/1¾ cups) dry breadcrumbs

oil, for deep-frying

TOMATO MAYONNAISE

90 ml (3 fl oz) tomato sauce (ketchup)

90 ml (3 fl oz) mayonnaise

½ teaspoon finely chopped dill or parsley

½ garlic clove, crushed

Prep time: 30 minutes
Cooking time: 5 minutes
Makes 12

Use a small sharp knife to separate the meat from the bones at the meaty end of each wing bone. Push the meat along the bone and fold it over the end of the bone to form a ball shape. Coat each piece lightly with cornflour, shaking off any excess, then dip into the egg white and coat with the breadcrumbs.

To make the tomato mayonnaise, combine the tomato sauce, mayonnaise, dill or parsley and garlic in a bowl until well combined.

Fill a saucepan two-thirds full with oil and heat to 170°C (325°F), or until a cube of bread dropped in the oil browns in 20 seconds. Cook half the drumsticks at a time in the hot oil for 2–3 minutes, or until golden and cooked through.

Drain on paper towels and serve with the tomato mayonnaise.

HINTS: Look for chicken drumettes in your supermarket to save time preparing the chicken wings. These mini drumsticks can also be served cold and make great picnic food.

mini quiche lorraines

These tasty little quiches make a filling meal. They are also a good source of calcium and phosphorus plus they provide vitamin A, D and the B vitamins.

2 sheets frozen ready-rolled shortcrust (pie) pastry, thawed

1 tomato, chopped

60 g (2¼ oz/½ cup) grated cheddar cheese

40 g (1½ oz/¼ cup) chopped ham or bacon

1 spring onion (scallion), finely chopped

125 ml (4 fl oz/½ cup) milk

1 egg

Prep time: 10 minutes

Cooking time: 15–20 minutes

Makes 12

Preheat the oven to 200°C (400°F/Gas 6).

Cut the pastry into 12 rounds using a 8 cm (3¼ inch) cutter. Line 12 shallow patty pans or mini muffin tins with the pastry.

Mix together the tomato, cheese, ham and spring onion and spoon the mixture into the pastry cases.

Whisk together the milk and egg. Pour enough into each pastry case to cover the filling.

Bake in the oven for 15–20 minutes, or until the filling is set and golden. Transfer to a wire rack to cool. Store in the refrigerator in an airtight container for up to 2 days.

variations: There are many different combinations of ingredients you can use to create your toddler's favourite quiche. Try semi-dried (sun-blushed) tomatoes, feta and thyme; chopped black olives, ricotta and chicken; and tinned salmon, capers and cream cheese.

fruit & vegetable salad with creamy cottage cheese

Getting toddlers to eat vegetables can be difficult. Mix vegetables with fruit and a tasty dressing and your toddler may surprise you. Don't despair if he only eats fruit, as both fruit and vegetables are rich in fibre and have similar vitamins.

50 g (1¾ oz/⅔ cup) dried fruit (apples, prunes, apricots, sultanas/golden raisins and raisins)

1 celery stalk, diced

1 orange or 2 mandarins, segmented

mixed salad leaves

DRESSING

125 g (4½ oz/½ cup) cottage or ricotta cheese

2 tablespoons cream (whipping)

Prep time: 15 minutes + 5 minutes standing

Cooking time: Nil

Serves 4

Cut the dried apple rings into quarters and the prunes and apricots into halves. Put the apples, prunes and apricots into a bowl and cover with boiling water. Leave to stand for 5 minutes. Drain, rinse under cold water and drain again.

Combine all the fruit with the diced celery and orange segments. Put the salad leaves in a bowl and arrange the fruit and vegetable mixture on the leaves.

To make the dressing, combine the cottage or ricotta cheese with the cream. Toss the dressing through the fruit and vegetable mix and serve.

instant mini pizzas

These pizzas are a quick lunch that your toddler can help you prepare. Let him spread on the tomato sauce or sprinkle over the cheese — this makes the pizzas an even more anticipated meal.

3 English muffins, split in half

unsalted butter or olive oil

3 tablespoons chunky tomato-based pasta sauce

90 g (3¼ oz) cooked ham, bacon or chicken, cut into strips

60 g (2¼ oz/½ cup) grated cheddar cheese

Prep time: 5 minutes
Cooking time: 10 minutes
Makes 6

Preheat the oven to 240°C (475°F/Gas 8). Lightly spread the muffin halves with butter or oil. Spread the tomato-based pasta sauce over the muffins, top with the strips of ham and cover with the cheese. Place onto a baking tray and bake for 8–10 minutes, or until the muffins are crisp and the cheese has melted and turned golden.

variations: Adult and older children's servings can be garnished with pineapple pieces, avocado chunks or olives before heating in the oven. Small sized pitta bread (pockets) can be used instead of muffins.

leek, zucchini & cheese frittata

This frittata combines the vegetables in a nourishing cheese and egg base, which is a great — if slightly sneaky — way of upping your toddler's vegetable intake.

2 tablespoons olive oil

3 leeks, thinly sliced (white part only)

2 zucchini (courgettes), cut into matchstick pieces

1 garlic clove, crushed

5 eggs, lightly beaten

4 tablespoons freshly grated parmesan cheese

4 tablespoons diced Swiss cheese

Prep time: 20 minutes

Cooking time: 40 minutes

Serves 4

Heat 1 tablespoon of the olive oil in small ovenproof pan. Add the leek and cook, stirring, over low heat until slightly softened. Cover and cook the leek for 10 minutes, stirring occasionally. Add the zucchini and garlic and cook for another 10 minutes. Transfer the mixture to a bowl. Allow to cool, then season with freshly ground black pepper. Add the egg and cheeses and stir through.

Heat the remaining oil in the pan, then add the egg mixture and smooth the surface. Cook over low heat for 15 minutes, or until the frittata is almost set.

Put the pan under a preheated hot grill (broiler) for 3–5 minutes, or until the top is set and golden. Allow the frittata to stand for 5 minutes before cutting into wedges and serving. Serve with a fresh green salad.

spanish omelette

This recipe is a great way to serve up potatoes, a little known source of vitamin C. It also makes a great picnic food that can be sliced up cold into bite-sized pieces for little ones or larger wedges for grown-ups.

1 kg (2 lb 4 oz) potatoes

2 large red (Spanish) onions, coarsely chopped

50 g (1¾ oz) unsalted butter

2 tablespoons olive oil

1 garlic clove, crushed

2 tablespoons finely chopped parsley

4 eggs, lightly beaten

Prep time: 20 minutes
Cooking time: 35 minutes
Serves 4–6

Cut the potatoes into small cubes and place in a large ovenproof saucepan. Cover with water, then bring to the boil and cook, uncovered, for 3 minutes. Remove the pan from the heat and allow to stand, covered, for 8 minutes, or until the potato is just tender. Drain well.

Heat the butter and oil in a deep, non-stick frying pan over medium heat. Add the onions and garlic and cook for 8 minutes, stirring occasionally. Add the potato and cook for another 5 minutes. Remove the vegetables with a slotted spoon and transfer them to a large bowl, reserving the oil in the frying pan. Add the parsley and eggs to the potato and onion and mix until well combined.

Reheat the oil in the frying pan over high heat and add the mixture. Reduce the heat to low and cook, covered, for about 10 minutes, or until the underside of the omelette is golden. Brown the top of the omelette under a hot grill (broiler).

corn & capsicum fritters

As with spanish omelette, this recipe can also be served up cold as part of a picnic. Try serving them with your toddler's favourite dipping sauce and see how much he enjoys these vegies!

1 large red capsicum (pepper)

2–3 cobs fresh corn kernels (about 300 g/10½ oz) or 300 g (10½ oz/1½ cups) tinned corn kernels, drained

oil, for frying

2 tablespoons chopped parsley, coriander (cilantro) leaves, chives or dill

3 eggs

Prep time: 20 minutes
Cooking time: 10 minutes
Serves 4

Cut the capsicum into large pieces, discarding the seeds and membrane, then chop into small pieces. Cut the kernels from the fresh corn, using a sharp knife. Heat 2 tablespoons oil in a frying pan. Add the corn and stir over medium heat for 2 minutes. Add the capsicum and stir for another 2 minutes. Transfer the vegetables to a bowl. Add the herbs and stir well to combine. Beat the eggs in a small bowl with a little freshly ground black pepper. Stir the egg gradually into the vegetable mixture.

Heat a non-stick frying pan over medium heat. Add enough oil to cover the base. Drop large spoonfuls of the vegetable mixture into the oil, a few at a time. Cook the fritters for 1–2 minutes, or until brown. Turn and cook the other side. Drain on paper towels and keep warm while you cook the remainder.

HINTS: These fritters may be served with sour cream and a green salad for lunch or as an accompaniment to a main course. Take care as these fritters contain no flour, so they cook quickly. You want them to still be a little creamy in the middle when done.

chickpea & parsley salad

Chickpeas are popular with toddlers because of their small size and yummy nut-like texture and taste. Chickpeas make a perfect meal, as they are a great source of vegetable protein, many vitamins and minerals, especially iron.

440 g (15½ oz/2 cups) tinned chickpeas

3 large tomatoes

2 tablespoons chopped parsley

2 teaspoons chopped mint

2 tablespoons lemon juice

2½ tablespoons plain yoghurt

Prep time: 10 minutes

Cooking time: Nil

Serves 4

Drain the chickpeas, rinse under cold running water and drain again. Chop the tomatoes into 1 cm (½ inch) pieces and put in a bowl with the drained chickpeas, parsley and mint.

In a small bowl, combine the lemon juice and yoghurt. Pour over the salad and mix until well combined.

vegetable filo pouches

This recipe makes a good meal for vegetarian toddlers, being rich in vegetable protein, vitamins and minerals. You can also add a variety of other vegetables.

oil spray

8 sheets filo pastry

80 g (2¾ oz/½ cup) sesame seeds

FILLING

450 g (1 lb/3 cups) grated carrot

2 large onions, finely chopped

1 tablespoon grated fresh ginger

1 tablespoon finely chopped coriander (cilantro) leaves

225 g (8 oz/1⅓ cups) tinned water chestnuts, rinsed and sliced

1 tablespoon white miso paste

3 tablespoons tahini paste

Prep time: 45 minutes

Cooking time: 35–40 minutes

Serves 4

Preheat the oven to 180°C (350°F/ Gas 4). Spray two baking trays with oil.

To make the filling, combine the carrot, onion, ginger, coriander and 250 ml (9 fl oz/1 cup) water in a large pan. Cover and cook over low heat for 20 minutes. Uncover, cook for a further 5 minutes, or until all the liquid has evaporated. Remove from the heat and cool slightly. Stir in the water chestnuts, miso and tahini.

Place one sheet of filo pastry on a work surface. Spray lightly with oil. Top with another three pastry sheets, spraying between each layer. Cut the pastry into six even squares. Repeat the process with the remaining pastry sheets giving 12 squares in total.

Divide the filling evenly between each square, placing the filling in the centre. Bring the edges together and pinch to form a pouch. Spray the lower portion of each pouch with oil, then press in the sesame seeds. Place the pouches on the prepared trays and bake for 10–12 minutes, or until golden brown and crisp. Serve hot with sweet chilli sauce, if desired.

You can assemble the pouches up to 1 day ahead and cook just before serving. Store in the refrigerator until needed.

bubble & squeak

This is a great way of turning leftovers into a tasty and nutritious meal rich in vitamins A, C and the B group, as well as potassium.

150 g (5½ oz/1 cup) cooked potato

150 g (5½ oz/1 cup) cooked pumpkin (winter squash)

50 g (1¾ oz/1 cup) grated cabbage, cooked

50 g (1¾ oz/1 cup) small broccoli florets, cooked

4 eggs, beaten

2 chives, snipped

20 g (¾ oz) unsalted butter

Prep time: 10 minutes
Cooking time: 5 minutes
Serves 4

Put the vegetables in a bowl and mix well with the egg and chives. Melt the butter in a large frying pan and add the vegetable mixture. Cook over medium heat until the underside is golden, then cut into quarters and turn. Cook the mixture for a little longer until the surface is golden and the egg set. Alternatively, once the underside is cooked, put the frying pan under a hot grill (broiler) for 1–2 minutes, or until the top is set.

HINTS: Any combination of left-over cooked vegetables can be used. Any left-over cooked meat can also be chopped and added to the mixture.

pork & chive dumplings

Tasty little surprise packages are fun to make. The pork makes them a good source of protein and the B vitamin thiamin.

I teaspoon vegetable oil

2 garlic cloves, crushed

2 teaspoons finely grated ginger

30 g (I oz/I bunch) chives, snipped

½ carrot, finely diced

200 g (7 oz) minced (ground) pork

2 tablespoons oyster sauce

3 teaspoons salt-reduced soy sauce

½ teaspoon sesame oil

I teaspoon cornflour (cornstarch)

24 round gow gee wrappers

Prep time: 45 minutes

Cooking time: 15 minutes

Makes 24

Heat a wok over high heat, add the vegetable oil and swirl to coat the side of the wok. Add the garlic, ginger, chives and carrot, then stir-fry for 2 minutes, or until fragrant. Remove the wok from the heat and allow to cool.

Meanwhile, put the pork, oyster sauce, soy sauce, sesame oil and cornflour in a bowl and mix well. Add the vegetable mixture once it has cooled, mixing it into the pork mixture until well combined.

Put 2 teaspoons of the mixture in the centre of a gow gee wrapper. Moisten the edges with water, then fold the sides together to form a semi-circle. Pinch the edges together at 5 mm (¼ inch) intervals to form a ruffled edge. Repeat with the remaining filling and wrappers. Line a double bamboo steamer with baking paper. Put half the dumplings in a single layer in each steamer basket. Cover and steam over a wok of simmering water for 12 minutes, or until cooked through.

tomato, tuna & white bean pasta

Keep an eye on the big picture when fussiness about the evening meal happens. With a protein and carbohydrate-rich lunch like this pasta under his belt, you have less to worry about if he is too tired for a substantial dinner.

25 g (1 oz/¼ cup) small shell pasta or other small pasta

90 g (3¼ oz/⅓ cup) chunky tomato-based pasta sauce

100 g (3½ oz) tinned tuna in spring water, drained

2 tablespoons drained, rinsed tinned cannellini beans

1 teaspoon chopped drained, rinsed capers in brine

1 teaspoon finely chopped fresh basil

Prep time: 5 minutes
Cooking time: 10 minutes
Serves 2

Cook the pasta in a saucepan of boiling water until *al dente*. Drain and keep warm.

Meanwhile put the pasta sauce, tuna, beans, capers and basil in a small saucepan and stir over medium heat for 1–2 minutes, or until heated through. Toss through the pasta to serve.

tuna, caper & bean sandwich

Children like what they know, so if they only ever get to know white bread that is all they will ever want. Expose them early onto a wide range of breads. Rye, wholemeal (whole-wheat), wholegrain and pitta pockets are all good bread choices.

100 g (3½ oz) tinned tuna in spring water, drained

1 teaspoon finely chopped drained, rinsed capers in brine

3 teaspoons whole-egg mayonnaise

2 teaspoons canned cannellini beans, mashed

bread of your choice

Prep: time: 5 minutes

Cooking time: Nil

Serves 1

Put the tuna, capers, mayonnaise and cannellini beans in a bowl and mix well.

Add to the bread of your choice.

dinner

At the end of the day you may have more time to relax and have some family time together — and this can include dinner. If dinner becomes a time for constant discipline it will not be a pleasurable experience for either your toddler or you. Parents have been known to get anxious about what their children don't eat, so it is important to remember that your toddler is the only one who knows when he has had enough.

Being concerned about your toddler's eating habits is a waste of time and energy — as long as there is a variety of healthy foods presented to the toddler at meal time and he is allowed to eat as much of what he likes, he will be healthy and happy. Tiredness is also an issue at dinnertime. Don't delay dinner if it can be helped, as an overtired and emotional toddler is not likely to eat even if he is hungry.

The evening meal is the beginning of wind-down time. Your toddler may need to have his bath as soon as you have cleared away the plates, or after a short, quiet playtime. Many toddlers need a milk drink and some need a small snack as well before they have their teeth cleaned and snuggle down for the all-important bedtime story.

dinner on the go

Don't be afraid to use convenience foods to make life quicker and easier; just check the label for unwanted extras (see page 21 for more information). Try some of the following suggestions:

• Fresh or frozen fish can be easily microwaved (or steamed) to serve with a cooked frozen vegetable medley.

• Pasta with sliced ham, cooked frozen peas and grated cheese.

• Scrambled eggs and oven-fried potato chips (French fries).

• Boil up some quick-cook noodles with a frozen vegetable medley. Serve with shredded barbecued (grilled) chicken tossed through.

• Boil up the quick-cook noodles and some frozen vegetables in low-salt or home-made chicken stock. Add some shredded barbecued (grilled) chicken for quick chicken noodle soup.

• Couscous with tinned tuna or salmon.

• Macaroni cheese (see the recipe on page 87).

crispy lentil balls

Dried red lentils are excellent as they are the quickest legume to cook.
Legumes are a good source of protein and vitamins, minerals and fibre.

125 g (4½ oz/½ cup) red lentils

2 bulb spring onions (scallions), chopped

1 garlic clove, crushed

½ teaspoon ground cumin

40 g (1½ oz/½ cup) fresh breadcrumbs

60 g (2¼ oz/½ cup) grated cheddar cheese

½ large zucchini (courgette), grated

70 g (2½ oz/½ cup) polenta

oil, for deep-frying

Prep time: 20 minutes
Cooking time: 15 minutes
Makes 15

Put the lentils in a saucepan and cover with water. Bring to the boil, reduce the heat to low, then cover and simmer for 10 minutes, or until the lentils are tender. Drain and rinse well under cold water.

Combine half the lentils in a food processor or blender with the spring onions and garlic. Process for 10 seconds, or until the mixture is pulpy. Transfer to a large bowl and add the remaining lentils, cumin, breadcrumbs, cheese and zucchini. Stir until combined.

Using your hands, roll level tablespoons of the mixture into balls and toss lightly in the polenta.

Heat the oil in a heavy-based pan. Gently lower half the balls into medium–hot oil. Cook for 1 minute, or until golden brown and crisp. Carefully remove from the oil with tongs or a slotted spoon and drain on paper towels. Repeat the process with the remaining balls. Serve hot with your favourite dipping sauce.

quick pasta with tomato sauce

This recipe can be reinvented many times over by using various combinations of vegetables and tuna, plus any one of a variety of pasta shapes.

1 tablespoon extra virgin olive oil

1 garlic clove, crushed

400 g (14 oz/2 cups) tinned diced Roma (plum) tomatoes

250 g (9 oz/2¾ cups) penne or farfalle (bow tie pasta)

1 tablespoon shaved parmesan cheese (optional)

Prep time: 5 minutes
Cooking time: 10 minutes
Serves 4

Heat the olive oil in a frying pan over medium heat. Cook the garlic, stirring constantly, for 30 seconds. Add the tomatoes and stir through. Reduce the heat to low and cook for a further 8–10 minutes, stirring occasionally, or until reduced.

Meanwhile, cook the pasta in a large saucepan of salted boiling water until *al dente*. Drain and return to the saucepan.

Add the cooked tomatoes to the pasta and stir them through. Spoon a small portion into a bowl and sprinkle with parmesan cheese, if desired.

variation: Stir through the tomato sauce a spoonful of mashed, drained tinned tuna (preferably in spring water, not oil or brine) and just cooked (not mushy) vegetables such as diced zucchini (courgettes), diced carrot, diced butternut pumpkin (squash), finely chopped English spinach and finely chopped flat-leaf (Italian) parsley.

simple bolognese

Most of us eat far too much salt, even young children. When preparing this dish use salt-reduced or no-added-salt tinned tomatoes, tomato paste and stock.

2 tablespoons olive oil

1 onion, finely chopped

1 garlic clove, crushed

500 g (1 lb 2 oz) minced (ground) beef

25 g (1 oz/¼ cup) chopped mushrooms

2 tablespoons tomato paste (concentrated purée)

425 g (15 oz/1¾ cups) tinned chopped tomatoes

125 ml (4 fl oz/½ cup) salt-reduced beef stock or water

1 tablespoon chopped parsley

cooked pasta of your choice

parmesan or cheddar cheese, grated

Prep time: 10 minutes
Cooking time: 30 minutes
Serves 8

Heat the oil in a heavy-based saucepan and sauté the onion and garlic until tender. Add the beef and brown well, breaking the meat up with a spoon as it cooks.

Add the chopped mushrooms to the saucepan and cook for 1 minute. Blend in the tomato paste.

Stir in the tomato, stock or water, parsley and season with freshly ground black pepper. Bring to the boil and then reduce the heat and simmer, stirring occasionally, for 20 minutes.

Toss the sauce through hot, drained pasta, such as spaghetti or linguine. Sprinkle with grated parmesan or cheddar cheese, if desired, and serve with a crisp green salad.

You can freeze the left-over sauce in portion sizes for up to 3 months.

mini shepherd's pies

The lean minced (ground) beef used in this recipe is not only easy for toddlers to chew, but will make a significant contribution to your toddler's iron intake.

1 tablespoon oil

500 g (1 lb 2 oz) minced (ground) steak

2 tablespoons plain (all-purpose) flour

250 ml (9 fl oz/1 cup) salt-reduced beef stock

2 tablespoons chopped parsley

4 potatoes, cooked

60 ml (2 fl oz/¼ cup) milk

15 g (½ oz) unsalted butter

270 g (9½ oz/2 cups) frozen mixed vegetables (peas, beans, carrots), thawed

60 g (2¼ oz/½ cup) grated cheese

25 g (1 oz/¼ cup) dried breadcrumbs

Prep time: 10 minutes
Cooking time: 30 minutes
Makes 4

Preheat the oven to 180°C (350°F/Gas 4). Heat the oil in a frying pan, add the meat and brown, breaking the meat up with a spoon as it cooks. Stir in the flour and cook, stirring, for 1 minute.

Blend in the stock, parsley and some freshly ground black pepper to taste. Simmer, stirring, for about 5 minutes, or until the mixture thickens.

Mash the potatoes well and beat until smooth with the milk and butter, adding more of each if needed.

Spoon the meat mixture into four small ramekin dishes. Top with an even amount of the mixed vegetables and spread the mashed potato over the top.

Mix together the cheese and breadcrumbs and sprinkle over each pie. Bake in the oven for 10–15 minutes, or until the tops are golden.

bean enchiladas

Make this an interactive meal — let your toddler assemble these himself — making it a fun 'hands on' meal. Don't forget to relax about the mess!

1 tablespoon light olive oil

1 onion, thinly sliced

3 garlic cloves, crushed

2 teaspoons ground cumin

125 ml (4 fl oz/½ cup) salt-reduced vegetable stock

3 tomatoes, peeled, deseeded and chopped

1 tablespoon tomato paste (concentrated purée)

850 g (1 lb 14 oz) tinned 3-bean mix

2 tablespoons chopped coriander (cilantro) leaves

8 flour tortillas

1 small avocado, chopped

125 g (4½ oz/½ cup) light sour cream

1 handful coriander (cilantro) sprigs

115 g (4 oz/2 cups) shredded lettuce

Prep time: 20 minutes

Cooking time: 25 minutes

Makes 8

Preheat the oven to 170°C (325°F/Gas 3).

Heat the oil in a deep frying pan over medium heat. Add the onion and cook for 3–4 minutes, or until just soft. Add the garlic and cook for a further 30 seconds. Add the cumin, vegetable stock, tomato and tomato paste and cook for 6–8 minutes, or until the mixture is quite thick and pulpy. Season with freshly ground black pepper.

Drain and rinse the 3-bean mix. Add the beans to the sauce and cook for 5 minutes to heat through, then add the chopped coriander.

Meanwhile, wrap the tortillas in foil and warm in the oven for 3–4 minutes.

Place a tortilla on a plate and spread with a large scoop of the bean mixture. Top with some avocado, sour cream, coriander sprigs and lettuce. Roll the enchiladas up, tucking in the ends. Cut each one in half to serve.

variations: For beef enchiladas, use only half the quantity of 3-bean mix and add 500 g (1 lb 2 oz) lean minced (ground) beef. Cook the beef with the garlic for 5–6 minutes, or until browned and cooked through, breaking up any lumps with the back of a spoon. Alternatively, for tuna enchiladas, use only half the quantity of 3-bean mix and add 425 g (15 oz) tinned tuna in brine, drained. Add the tuna with the stock.

vegetable & noodle stir-fry

Protein is an important part of a growing child's diet. Main meals for vegetarian children should always include a vegetable protein such as tofu.

50 g (1¾ oz) cellophane or egg noodles

2 teaspoons oil

1 carrot, chopped

1 celery stalk, chopped

1 small zucchini (courgette), halved lenthways, sliced

½ red capsicum (pepper), deseeded, chopped

60 g (2¼ oz/½ cup) cauliflower florets

30 g (1 oz/½ cup) broccoli florets

30 g (1 oz/¼ cup) sliced green beans

½ garlic clove, crushed

2 teaspoons salt-reduced soy sauce

Prep time: 10 minutes

Cooking time: 7 minutes

Serves 4

Place the noodles in a bowl. Cover with boiling water. Leave to stand for 1 minute, or until tender. Drain.

Heat the oil in a wok or frying pan. Add the carrot, celery, zucchini, capsicum, cauliflower, broccoli, beans and garlic and stir-fry for 4–5 minutes.

Toss the noodles through the vegetables with the soy sauce. Stir-fry for 1 minute. Serve immediately.

variation: To make this a more substantial meal, cut 200 g (7 oz) silken firm tofu into 2 cm (¾ inch) cubes or grate 200 g (7 oz) hard tofu and add to the stir-fry after cooking the vegetables. Gently toss through for 1 minute to heat through. If adding tofu, reduce the amount of vegetables.

fried rice

Using frozen foods won't compromise your family's nutrition. That's because their cooking and freezing are so quick that loss of important nutrients is small. This means more vitamins for everyone.

2 tablespoons peanut oil

2 eggs, well beaten

4 slices rindless bacon, chopped

2 teaspoons finely grated fresh ginger

1 garlic clove, crushed

6 spring onions (scallions), finely chopped

50 g (1¾ oz) red capsicum (pepper), deseeded and diced

1 teaspoon sesame oil

750 g (1 lb 10 oz/4 cups) cooked, cold, long-grain white rice (see Hint)

100 g (3½ oz/⅔ cup) frozen peas, thawed

100 g (3½ oz) cooked, chopped chicken

2 tablespoons salt-reduced soy sauce

Prep time: 25 minutes
Cooking time: 10 minutes
Serves 4

Heat a large heavy-based wok until very hot, add about 2 teaspoons of the peanut oil and swirl. Pour in the eggs and swirl to coat the side of the wok. Cook until just set. Remove from the wok, roll up and set aside. Add the remaining oil to the wok and stir-fry the bacon for 2 minutes. Add the ginger, garlic, spring onion and capsicum and stir-fry for 2 minutes.

Add the sesame oil and the rice. Stir-fry, tossing regularly, until the rice is heated through.

Cut the egg into thin strips and add to wok with the peas and the chicken. Cover and steam for 1 minute, or until everything is heated through. Stir in the soy sauce and serve.

HINT: White rice almost triples in bulk during cooking so you will need about 250 g (9 oz/1¼ cups) uncooked rice to give 750 g (1 lb 10 oz/4 cups) cooked rice. Alternatively, you can buy pre-cooked frozen rice. Ensure it is thawed before using it in this recipe.

chickpea curry

Until recently, spicy foods were considered a no no for children. But with the exception of hot spices like chilli and cayenne, there is no reason why your older baby or toddler can't experience the wonderful flavours of the world.

1 tablespoon oil

2 onions, thinly sliced

4 garlic cloves, crushed

1 teaspoon turmeric

1 teaspoon paprika

1 tablespoon ground cumin

1 tablespoon ground coriander

875 g (1 lb 15 oz/4 cups) tinned chickpeas, drained

440 g (15½ oz/1¾ cups) tinned chopped tomatoes

1 teaspoon garam masala

Prep time: 15 minutes

Cooking time: 35 minutes

Serves 4

Heat the oil in a saucepan over medium heat. Add the onion and garlic to the pan and cook, stirring, until soft.

Add the turmeric, paprika, cumin and coriander. Stir for 1 minute.

Add the chickpeas and tomato, and stir until combined. Simmer, covered, over low heat for 20 minutes, stirring occasionally. Stir in the garam masala, then simmer, covered, for another 10 minutes. Serve with steamed rice.

HINT: This curry also makes a delicious meal wrapped inside chapattis or naan bread.

chinese-style steamed fish on vegetables

Iodine is an essential nutrient for humans, both large and small, and both fish and seafood are excellent sources.

1 carrot, cut into 5 cm (2 inch) matchstick strips

½ celery stalk, cut into 5 cm (2 inch) matchstick strips

2 small spring onions (scallions), cut into 5 cm (2 inch) matchstick strips

4 mushrooms, cut into matchstick strips

4 boneless white fish fillets (about 400 g/14 oz), skin on

2 teaspoons salt-reduced soy sauce

2 teaspoons vegetable oil

Prep time: 10 minutes
Cooking time: 10 minutes
Serves 4

Put the vegetable strips on a dish that will fit in a steamer. Arrange the fish, skin side up, on the vegetables. Combine the soy sauce and vegetable oil together, then pour over the fish. Place the dish in a steamer, cover, and steam over simmering water for about 10 minutes, or until the fish flakes when tested with a fork.

HINT: To cook this dish in the oven, arrange the ingredients, as above, on a rack in an ovenproof dish and add 60–125 ml (2–4 fl oz/¼–½ cup) water. Cover and bake in a preheated 180°C (350°F/Gas 4) oven for 15 minutes, or until the fish flakes easily and is cooked through.

beef stroganoff

Stroganoff is a hearty and tasty winter meal that is a good source of protein and the minerals iron and zinc.

500 g (1 lb 2 oz) lean rump steak

2 tablespoons plain (all-purpose) flour

50 g (1¾ oz) unsalted butter

1 large onion, sliced

1 garlic clove, crushed

150 g (5½ oz) mushrooms, sliced

185 ml (6 fl oz/¾ cup) salt-reduced beef stock

1 tablespoon tomato paste (concentrated purée)

185 g (6½ oz/¾ cup) sour cream

1 tablespoon finely chopped flat-leaf (Italian) parsley

Prep time: 15 minutes
Cooking time: 15 minutes
Serves 4

Cut the beef into strips and place it and the flour in a plastic bag and toss to coat, shaking off any excess. Heat half the butter in a large frying pan and cook the onion and garlic for 2 minutes, or until golden. Add the mushrooms and cook for a further 3 minutes, then remove from the pan.

Heat the remaining butter in the same frying pan, add the beef in batches and cook over medium–high heat for 3–4 minutes, or until browned. Return the onion and mushroom mixture and all the beef to the pan with any juices.

Stir in the stock and tomato paste, bring to the boil, then reduce the heat and simmer for 2–3 minutes. Add the sour cream and half the chopped parsley and season to taste with freshly ground black pepper. Mix together well, then serve immediately with steamed rice. Garnish with the remaining parsley.

niçoise salad

Tinned tuna is a tasty, nutritious food, rich in the omega-3 fats that are such good brain food for growing children. The best choices are those packed in a good oil (such as olive, canola or sunflower oil) or spring water.

3 eggs

125 ml (4 fl oz/½ cup) olive oil

2 tablespoons white wine vinegar

1 garlic clove, crushed

325 g (11½ oz) iceberg lettuce, shredded

12 cherry tomatoes, cut into quarters

175 g (6 oz/1½ cups) baby green beans, trimmed and blanched

1 small red capsicum (pepper), deseeded and thinly sliced

1 celery stalk, cut into 5 cm (2 inch) strips

1 Lebanese (short) cucumber, deseeded, cut into 5 cm (2 inch) strips

375 g (13 oz) tinned tuna, drained and flaked

12 stoned kalamata olives, halved

4 anchovy fillets, finely chopped (optional)

Prep time: 20 minutes

Cooking time: 10 minutes

Serves 4

Put the eggs in a saucepan of cold water. Bring slowly to the boil, then reduce the heat and simmer for 10 minutes. Stir the water during the first few minutes to centre the yolk. Drain and cool under cold water, then peel and cut into quarters.

Combine the oil, vinegar and garlic in a small bowl and mix well. Put the lettuce, tomato, beans, capsicum, celery, cucumber, tuna, olives and anchovies in a large bowl. Pour over the dressing and toss well to combine. Serve the salad topped with the egg quarters.

baked chicken & leek risotto

Rice is a great food for kids to demonstrate their developing cutlery technique. It's still a messy business at this stage, so be patient!

60 g (2¼ oz) unsalted butter

1 leek, thinly sliced

2 boneless, skinless chicken breasts, finely chopped

440 g (15½ oz/2 cups) risotto rice

60 ml (2 fl oz/¼ cup) white wine

1.25 litres (44 fl oz/5 cups) salt-reduced chicken stock

35 g (1¼ oz/⅓ cup) grated parmesan cheese, plus extra, to garnish

2 tablespoons thyme, plus extra, to garnish

Prep time: 10 minutes

Cooking time: 40 minutes

Serves 4–6

Preheat the oven to 150°C (300°F/Gas 2). Heat the butter in a 5 litre (175 fl oz/20 cup) ovenproof dish with a lid over medium heat, add the leek and cook for 2 minutes, or until softened but not browned.

Add the chicken and cook, stirring, for 2–3 minutes, or until it is golden on both sides. Add the rice and stir so that it is well coated with butter. Cook for 1 minute.

Add the wine and stock and bring to the boil. Cover and place in the oven and cook for 30 minutes, stirring halfway through. Remove from the oven and stir through the parmesan and thyme leaves. Season with freshly ground black pepper. Sprinkle with the extra thyme and parmesan and serve.

lamb kofta curry

This curry is a great introduction to the tastes of India for your toddler. Just be certain the curry paste you buy is a mild one.

500 g (1 lb 2 oz) lean minced (ground) lamb

1 onion, finely chopped

1 garlic clove, crushed

1 teaspoon grated fresh ginger

1 teaspoon garam masala

1 teaspoon ground coriander

40 g (1½ oz/⅓ cup) ground almonds

steamed rice, to serve

SAUCE

2 teaspoons oil

1 onion, finely chopped

3 tablespoons mild Korma curry paste

400 g (14 oz/2 cups) tinned chopped tomatoes

125 g (4½ oz/½ cup) plain yoghurt

1 teaspoon lemon juice

Prep time: 25 minutes
Cooking time: 35 minutes
Serves 4

Combine the lamb, onion, garlic, ginger, garam masala, ground coriander and ground almonds in a bowl. Shape the mixture into walnut-sized balls with your hands.

Heat a large non-stick frying pan and cook the koftas in batches until brown on both sides — they don't have to be cooked all the way through at this stage.

Meanwhile, to make the sauce, heat the oil in a saucepan over low heat. Add the onion and cook for 6–8 minutes, or until soft and golden. Add the curry paste and cook for 1 minute, or until fragrant. Add the chopped tomato and simmer for 5 minutes. Stir in the yoghurt (1 tablespoon at a time) and the lemon juice until combined.

Place the koftas in the tomato sauce. Cook, covered, over low heat for 20 minutes. Serve over steamed rice.

pea & ham risotto

Green peas are a good source of vegetable protein and fibre. Their sweet flavour and bright colour also makes them a hit with small children.

1 tablespoon olive oil

1 celery stalk, chopped

2 tablespoons chopped flat-leaf (Italian) parsley

70 g (2½ oz) sliced ham, coarsely chopped

250 g (9 oz/1⅔ cups) peas (fresh or frozen)

125 ml (4 fl oz/½ cup) dry white wine

750 ml (26 fl oz/3 cups) salt-reduced chicken stock

60 g (2¼ oz) unsalted butter

1 onion, chopped

440 g (15½ oz/2 cups) risotto rice

35 g (1¼ oz/⅓ cup) grated parmesan cheese, plus extra shavings, to garnish

Prep time: 25 minutes

Cooking time: 45 minutes

Serves 4

Heat the oil in a frying pan, add the celery and parsley and season with freshly ground black pepper. Cook over medium heat for a few minutes to soften the celery. Add the ham and stir for 1 minute. Add the peas and half the wine, bring to the boil, then reduce the heat and simmer, uncovered, until almost all the liquid has evaporated. Set aside.

Put the stock and 750 ml (26 fl oz/3 cups) water in a separate saucepan and keep at simmering point.

Heat the butter in a large heavy-based saucepan. Add the onion and stir until softened. Add the rice and stir well. Pour in the remaining wine; allow it to bubble and evaporate. Add 125 ml (4 fl oz/½ cup) hot stock to the rice mixture. Stir constantly over low heat, with a wooden spoon, until all the stock has been absorbed. Repeat the process until all the stock has been added and the rice is creamy and tender (it may take about 20–25 minutes).

Add the pea mixture and parmesan and serve immediately. Serve with the extra parmesan shavings and some freshly ground black pepper.

HINT: If fresh peas are in season, 500 g (1 lb 2 oz) peas in the pod will yield about 250 g (9 oz/1⅔ cups) shelled peas.

toddler's chilli con carne

Research tells us that the foundations of a child's food preferences are established in the early days of eating. Don't be afraid to allow them to try new and tasty flavours; the experience will pay off when they are older.

2 teaspoons olive oil

1 large onion, chopped

1 garlic clove, crushed

2 teaspoons sweet paprika

1 teaspoon dried oregano

2 teaspoons ground cumin

750 g (1 lb 10 oz) lean minced (ground) beef

375 ml (13 fl oz/1½ cups) salt-reduced beef stock

400 g (14 oz/2 cups) tinned diced tomatoes

125 g (4½ oz/½ cup) tomato paste (concentrated purée)

300 g (10½ oz) tinned kidney beans, drained and rinsed

Prep time: 15 minutes

Cooking time: 1 hour 10 minutes

Serves 6

Heat the olive oil in a large saucepan over low heat. Add the onion and cook for 4–5 minutes, or until soft. Stir in the garlic, paprika, oregano and cumin. Increase the heat to medium, add the beef and cook for 5–8 minutes, or until just browned, breaking up any lumps with a spoon.

Reduce the heat to low, add the stock, tomato and tomato paste to the pan and cook for 35–45 minutes, stirring frequently.

Stir in the kidney beans and simmer for 10 minutes. Serve on its own or over rice.

baked chicken nuggets

This recipe is great competition for its fast food counterparts because it uses premium ingredients that are nutritious, tasty and fun to eat.

40 g (1½ oz/1⅓ cups) corn-based cereal flakes

400 g (14 oz) boneless, skinless chicken breasts

plain (all-purpose) flour, for dusting

1 egg white

Prep time: 15 minutes
Cooking time: 10 minutes
Serves 4

Preheat the oven to 200°C (400°F/Gas 6). Process the corn-based cereal flakes in a food processor, blender or in a mortar with a pestle, to make fine crumbs.

Cut the chicken breasts into bite-sized pieces. Toss in seasoned flour then in lightly beaten egg white. Roll each piece in the cereal-flake crumbs until well coated.

Lightly grease a baking tray with oil and place the nuggets on it. Bake for 10 minutes, or until golden and cooked through.

baked potato wedges

Preheat the oven to 200°C (400°F/Gas 6). Peel and slice 1.3 kg (3 lb) orange sweet potato into 6 x 2 cm (2½ x ¾ inch) wedges. Put the sweet potato wedges in a large roasting tin and toss with 2 tablespoons of olive oil. Bake for about 30 minutes, or until browned and crisp. Serve warm. Serves 4.

battered fish & chunky wedges

Full of the good fats important for brain development, fish should be a weekly part of the family menu. Firm white fish is a good choice for this recipe.

3 all-purpose potatoes

polyunsaturated oil, for deep-frying

125 g (4½ oz/1 cup) self-raising flour

1 egg, beaten

185 ml (6 fl oz/¾ cup) beer

4 white fish fillets

plain (all-purpose) flour, for dusting

125 g (4½ oz/½ cup) ready-made tartare sauce

Prep time: 15 minutes

Cooking time: 15 minutes

Serves 4

Wash the potatoes, but do not peel them. Cut into thick wedges, then dry with paper towels. Fill a large heavy-based saucepan two-thirds full with oil and heat. Gently lower the potato wedges into medium–hot oil. Cook for 4 minutes, or until tender and lightly browned. Carefully remove the wedges from the oil with a slotted spoon and drain on paper towels.

Sift the self-raising flour with some freshly ground black pepper into a large bowl and make a well in the centre. Add the egg and beer. Using a wooden spoon, stir until just combined and smooth. Dust the fish fillets in the plain flour, shaking off the excess. Add the fish fillets one at a time to the batter and toss until well coated. Remove the fish from the batter, draining off the excess batter.

Working with one piece of fish at a time, gently lower it into the medium–hot oil. Cook for 2 minutes, or until golden and crisp and cooked through. Carefully remove from the oil with a slotted spoon. Drain on paper towels, and keep warm while you cook the remainder. Return the potato wedges to the medium–hot oil. Cook for another 2 minutes, or until golden brown and crisp. Remove from the oil with a slotted spoon and drain on paper towels. Serve the wedges immediately with the fish and tartare sauce. If desired, serve with wedges of lemon and garnish with fresh dill.

HINTS: Old potatoes can be used in this recipe. Be sure to wash them well if you don't peel them. The beer can be fizzy or flat.

variation: You can serve the wedges with sour cream and sweet chilli sauce instead of tartare sauce.

chicken pilaf

Barbecued (grilled) chickens are a quick and healthy way to add protein to a meal — especially once you have removed the skin.

1 barbecued (grilled) chicken

50 g (1¾ oz) butter

1 onion, finely chopped

2 garlic cloves, crushed

300 g (10½ oz/1½ cups) basmati rice

1 tablespoon currants

2 tablespoons finely chopped dried apricots

1 teaspoon ground cinnamon

pinch of ground cardamom

750 ml (26 fl oz/3 cups) salt-reduced chicken stock

1 small handful coriander (cilantro) leaves, chopped

Prep time: 15 minutes

Cooking time: 20 minutes

Serves 4

Remove the skin and any fat from the chicken and chop the meat into even, bite-sized pieces.

Melt the butter in a large, deep frying pan over medium heat. Add the onion and garlic and cook for 2 minutes. Add the rice, currants, apricots and spices and stir until well coated.

Pour in the stock and bring to the boil. Reduce the heat to low and simmer, covered, for 15 minutes. Add a little water if it starts to dry out.

Stir through the chicken for 1–2 minutes, or until heated through, then stir through the coriander just before serving.

vegetable couscous

Couscous is a great staple for any family's pantry. It is made from durum wheat and is already pre-steamed, so it needs only a few minutes to cook.

30 g (1 oz) unsalted butter

1 onion, sliced

1 garlic clove, crushed

1 teaspoon ground cumin

2 carrots, thinly sliced

150 g (5½ oz) pumpkin (winter squash), chopped

300 g (10½ oz/1⅓ cups) tinned chickpeas, rinsed and drained

400 g (14 oz/2 cups) tinned chopped tomatoes

1 potato, chopped

1 small eggplant (aubergine), chopped

60 ml (2 fl oz/¼ cup) salt-reduced vegetable stock

150 g (5½ oz/1¼ cups) green beans, cut into short lengths

2 zucchini (courgettes), cut into chunks

COUSCOUS

250 ml (9 fl oz/1 cup) salt-reduced vegetable stock

185 g (6½ oz/1 cup) instant couscous

30 g (1 oz) unsalted butter

Prep time: 20 minutes

Cooking time: 30 minutes

Serves 4

Melt the butter in a saucepan over medium heat. Add the onion, garlic and cumin and cook for 2–3 minutes, or until softened.

Add the carrot, pumpkin, chickpeas, tomato, potato, eggplant and vegetable stock. Cook for 10 minutes, stirring occasionally. Mix in the beans and zucchini and cook for a further 5 minutes, or until the vegetables are tender.

To make the couscous, pour the stock and 60 ml (2 fl oz/¼ cup) water into a saucepan and bring to the boil. Remove from the heat and stir in the couscous and butter. Cover and stand for 5 minutes. Fluff the grains with a fork to separate. Serve the couscous topped with the vegetables, or fold the vegetables through the couscous.

fresh spring rolls

Letting children be involved in preparing and selecting their food can increase their desire to eat it. So for a fun meal, let everyone wrap their own rolls.

½ barbecued (grilled) chicken (see Hints)

50 g (1¾ oz) dried mung bean vermicelli

8 x 17 cm (6½ inch) square dried rice paper wrappers

16 Thai basil leaves

1 large handful coriander (cilantro) leaves

1 carrot, cut into short thin strips and blanched

2 tablespoons plum sauce

Prep time: 30 minutes

Cooking time: Nil

Makes 8

Remove the meat from the chicken carcass, discard the skin and finely shred. Soak the vermicelli in the hot water for 10 minutes and then drain. Dip a rice paper wrapper into warm water until it softens then place it on a clean work surface. Put one-eighth of the chicken in the centre of the wrapper and top with 2 basil leaves, a few coriander leaves, a few carrot strips and a small amount of vermicelli. Spoon a little plum sauce over the top.

Press the filling down to flatten it a little, then fold in the two sides and roll it up tightly like a parcel. Lay the roll seam side down, on a serving plate and sprinkle with a little water. Cover with a damp tea towel (dish towel) and repeat the process with the remaining ingredients. Serve with your favourite dipping sauce or a little extra plum sauce.

HINTS: When buying the barbecued (grilled) chicken, ask for two breast quarters. Rice paper wrappers must be kept moist or they become brittle. If you leave the spring rolls for any length of time and they start to dry out, sprinkle cold water on them.

chicken & mushroom spirals

Recipes that can be prepared ahead, like this one, are a blessing when dealing with small children. As every parent knows, timing is everything.

1 tablespoon olive oil

20 g (¾ oz) unsalted butter

2 slices rindless bacon, cut into thin strips

2 garlic cloves, crushed

250 g (9 oz) mushrooms, sliced

125 ml (4 fl oz/½ cup) dry white wine

185 ml (6 fl oz/¾ cup) cream (whipping)

4 spring onions (scallions), chopped

1 tablespoon plain (all-purpose) flour

2 large cooked boneless, skinless chicken breasts, chopped

500 g (1 lb 2 oz) spiral pasta

50 g (1¾ oz/½ cup) grated parmesan cheese

Prep time: 10 minutes

Cooking time: 20 minutes

Serves 4

Heat the oil and butter in a large, deep frying pan over medium heat. Add the bacon, garlic and mushrooms and cook for 2 minutes.

Add the wine and cook until the liquid has reduced by half. Add the cream and spring onions, and bring to the boil. Combine the flour and 60 ml (2 fl oz/¼ cup) water until smooth. Add to the pan and stir over the heat until the mixture boils and thickens. Reduce the heat and simmer for 1 minute. Fold through the chicken and cook for 1 minute to heat through. Season with freshly ground black pepper.

Cook the pasta in a large saucepan of boiling water, following the packet directions. Drain. Add the pasta to the sauce and toss to mix. Sprinkle with parmesan. Serve with a green salad.

HINTS: Scrub cutting boards thoroughly in hot soapy water to remove all traces of chicken. Make sure wooden boards have a smooth surface. Rough, cracked surfaces can contain bacteria. This sauce can be made 1 day in advance. Reheat the sauce and cook the pasta until al dente, just before serving.

veal schnitzel

Crumb the veal while your toddler is sleeping and this becomes another quick and nutritious meal to serve up with his favourite vegetables.

4 thin veal steaks

100 g (3⅓ oz/1 cup) dry breadcrumbs

½ teaspoon dried basil (optional)

25 g (1 oz/¼ cup) grated parmesan cheese

plain (all-purpose) flour, for coating

1 egg, lightly beaten

1 tablespoon milk

oilve oil, for frying

Prep time: 20 minutes + 30 minutes chilling

Cooking time: 5 minutes

Serves 4

Trim the meat of any excess fat. Place the veal between sheets of plastic wrap and flatten with a meat mallet or rolling pin until 3 mm (⅛ inch) thick. Nick the edges to prevent curling. Combine the breadcrumbs, basil, if using, and parmesan on a sheet of baking paper.

Coat the veal steaks in flour, shaking off the excess. Combine the beaten egg and milk. Working with one at a time, dip the steaks into the egg mixture, then coat with the breadcrumb mixture. Lightly shake off the excess. Refrigerate for 30 minutes to firm the coating.

Heat the oil in a large frying pan and cook the veal steaks over medium heat for 2–3 minutes on each side, or until golden and cooked through. Drain on paper towels and serve.

gado gado

Rich in protein from the eggs, beta-carotene from the carrots and sweet potato and vitamin C from the cabbage, gado gado is a nutritious adventure for toddlers.

3 eggs

2 orange sweet potatoes, cut into 1 cm (½ inch) thick slices

2 potatoes, halved and cut into 1 cm (½ inch) thick slices

125 g (4½ oz) baby (pattypan) squash, halved

250 g (9 oz) cabbage, cut into large pieces

2 carrots, cut into 1 cm (½ inch) thick strips

1 cucumber

125 g (4½ oz/1⅓ cups) fresh bean sprouts, tails removed

Prep time: 20 minutes

Cooking time: 20 minutes

Serves 6

Put the eggs in a saucepan with cold water to cover. Bring to the boil, reduce to a simmer and cook for 10 minutes; stir the water during the first few minutes to centre the yolk. Drain and cool under cold water.

Bring a large saucepan of water to the boil. Blanch each type of vegetable separately in the boiling water; they must be firm and not overcooked. The sweet potato and potato will each need about 8–10 minutes; the squash 1 minute; the carrots 2 minutes; and the cabbage 2 minutes. Remove the vegetables from the water with a slotted spoon and plunge into a bowl of iced water to stop the cooking process and set the colour.

Drain the vegetables from the iced water and dry briefly on paper towels. Shell the boiled eggs and cut them into quarters. Slice the cucumber into thin strips. Arrange all the vegetables in decorative groups and garnish with the sliced eggs and bean sprouts. Top with peanut sauce (see below).

peanut sauce

Heat 1 tablespoon oil in a saucepan and cook 1 finely chopped small onion for 5 minutes over low heat, or until soft and lightly golden. Add 125 g (4½ oz/½ cup) smooth peanut butter, 185 ml (6 fl oz/¾ cup) coconut milk, 1 tablespoon lemon juice, 1 tablespoon salt-reduced dark soy sauce and 60 ml (2 fl oz/¼ cup) water, and stir well. Bring to the boil, stirring constantly, then reduce the heat and simmer for 5 minutes, or until the sauce has reduced and thickened.

lamb cutlets with potato & pea mash

Meat on the bone is tender, tasty and particularly popular with toddlers. Finely chop the meat for those reluctant chewers but leave some meat remaining on the bone for them to gnaw off.

MASH

100 g (3½ oz) small new potatoes, chopped

½ small garlic clove, chopped

40 g (1½ oz/¼ cup) frozen peas

5 g (⅛ oz) unsalted butter

1 tablespoon milk

2 teaspoons oil

2 French trimmed lamb cutlets

Prep time: 5 minutes

Cooking time: 5 minutes

Serves 1

Bring a small saucepan of water to the boil and cook the potato and garlic for 4 minutes. Add the peas and cook for a further 1 minute or until the potato is soft. Drain, return to the saucepan and mash with the butter. Stir through the milk and keep warm.

Meanwhile, heat the oil in a small frying pan and cook the cutlets over medium heat for 2 minutes. Turn and cook for a further 1 minute, or until done to your liking. Serve with the mash.

HINT: Some toddlers will use the cutlet bone as a handle and chew the meat away from the bone. For smaller toddlers remove the meat from the bone, chop into small pieces and stir through the mash.

chicken & vegetable star pasta

Quick pasta meals like this are a good choice when hungry tummies are rumbling. It is also good for beta-carotene, protein and energy-giving carbohydrates.

2 tablespoons small star pasta or other small pasta

2 teaspoons oil

½ small onion, finely chopped

½ small garlic clove, crushed

60 g (2¼ oz) minced (ground) chicken

2 tablespoons grated zucchini (courgette)

2 tablespoons grated carrot

1½ tablespoons ricotta cheese

Prep time: 5 minutes
Cooking time: 10 minutes
Serves 2

Cook the pasta in boiling water for 5 minutes or until *al dente*. Drain and keep warm.

Heat the oil in a small saucepan and cook the onion and garlic over medium heat for 2–3 minutes, or until soft. Add the chicken and cook for 2–3 minutes, breaking up any lumps with a spoon. Add the zucchini and carrot and cook for 2 minutes, or until softened. Stir through the ricotta and pasta until well combined and warmed through.

spinach & ricotta cannelloni

Make an activity of meal preparation to keep toddlers happily occupied —
let them stir the filling, peel the onion or wash the spinach.

FILLING

20 g (¾ oz) unsalted butter
1 small onion, finely chopped
2 garlic cloves, crushed
3 bunches English spinach
300 g (10½ oz/1¼ cups) ricotta
1 tablespoon oregano

SAUCE

1 tablespoon olive oil
1 small onion, finely chopped
2 garlic cloves, crushed
440 g (15½ oz/1¾ cups) tinned
peeled whole tomatoes
125 ml (4 fl oz/½ cup) tomato-
based pasta sauce
1 teaspoon dried oregano
2 teaspoons Dijon mustard
1 tablespoon balsamic vinegar
1 teaspoon sugar

375 g (13 oz) fresh lasagne
70 g (2½ oz/½ cup) grated
mozzarella cheese
50 g (1¾ oz/½ cup) finely
grated parmesan cheese

Prep time: 45 minutes
Cooking time: 1 hour
Serves 4

Preheat the oven to 180°C (350°F/Gas 4).

To make the filling, melt the butter in a pan and add the onion and garlic. Cook for 3–5 minutes, or until the onion softens. Trim and finely shred the spinach, add it to the pan and cook for 5 minutes, or until wilted and the moisture has evaporated. Remove from the heat. Once cooled, combine with the ricotta and oregano in a food processor or blender. Process until smooth and season.

To make the sauce, heat the oil in a pan, add the onion and garlic and cook over low heat for 8–10 minutes. Add the rest of the sauce ingredients. Bring to the boil, then reduce the heat and simmer for 10–15 minutes, or until the sauce thickens.

Cut the lasagne sheets into twelve 12 cm (4½ inch) squares. Lightly grease a 2 litre (70 fl oz/8 cup) ovenproof dish. Spread one-third of the sauce over the base, then spoon 1½ tablespoons of the spinach mixture onto one side of each square of lasagne, leaving a 5 mm (¼ inch) border. Roll up the pasta to cover the filling and place in the dish seam side down. Repeat with all the sheets, spacing the cannelloni evenly in the dish. Spoon over the remaining sauce and sprinkle with the cheeses. Bake for 30–35 minutes, or until the cheese is bubbling and golden. Allow to stand for 5 minutes before serving.

sausages with parsnip & cauliflower purée

Sausages often get a bad rap but kids always seem to love them. Try to shop for sausages which contain lean meat, little salt and few, if any, additives.

PUREE

125 ml (4 fl oz/½ cup) salt-reduced vegetable or chicken stock

50 g (1¾ oz) parsnip, chopped

50 g (1¾ oz) cauliflower, cut into small florets

½ small garlic clove, chopped

2 teaspoons oil

2 chipolata sausages, or other small sausages

Prep time: 5 minutes

Cooking time: 5 minutes

Serves 1

To make the purée, put the stock in a small saucepan and bring to the boil. Add the parsnip, cauliflower and garlic, cover and cook for 5 minutes, or until the vegetables are soft. Drain, reserving the liquid. Place the vegetables in a small food processor and process until smooth, adding enough liquid to achieve the required consistency. Keep warm.

Meanwhile, heat the oil in a small frying pan and cook the sausages over medium heat for 3–4 minutes, turning until cooked through.

Cut the sausages into slices and serve as finger food with the mash or chop up and stir through the mash to be spoon fed.

potato & egg salad

This delicious salad is an excellent source of protein, fibre and carbohydrate, and also provides useful amounts of most vitamins and minerals. You can also prepare this salad ahead of time and store in the refrigerator.

I egg

I new potato, cut into 1.5 cm (⅝ inch) cubes

1½ tablespoons frozen peas, thawed

1 tablespoon drained tinned corn kernels

2 teaspoons finely diced celery

½ teaspoon finely chopped parsley

½ small garlic clove, crushed (optional)

2 teaspoons whole-egg mayonnaise

Prep time: 10 minutes
Cooking time: 10 minutes
Serves 1

Put the egg in a small saucepan of water and bring to the boil. Cook for 2 minutes, then add the potato and cook for a further 8 minutes. Drain. Rinse the egg under cold running water, peel and roughly chop.

Put the potato, egg, peas, corn, celery, parsley, garlic and mayonnaise in a small bowl and mix to combine. Season to taste.

osso buco

Take advantage of daytime sleeps to get this recipe on the stove — come dinnertime, all that needs to be done is the accompaniments. Osso buco is rich in protein, vitamins and the minerals iron and zinc.

8 large veal shanks, sliced

plain (all-purpose) flour, for dusting

20 g (¾ oz) unsalted butter

60 ml (2 fl oz/¼ cup) oil

1 onion, finely chopped

1 carrot, finely diced

1 celery stalk, finely diced

1 bay leaf

2 garlic cloves, crushed

250 ml (9 fl oz/1 cup) red wine (optional)

1 litre (35 fl oz/4 cups) salt-reduced beef stock

400 g (14 oz/2 cups) tinned diced tomatoes

Prep time: 20 minutes

Cooking time: 2 hours 50 minutes

Serves 6

Lightly dust the veal shanks in flour, shaking off the excess. Heat the butter and 2 tablespoons of the oil in a large heavy-based saucepan or casserole dish over high heat. Add the veal and cook in two batches for 2–3 minutes on each side, or until golden. Remove from the pan.

Reduce the heat to low and add the remaining oil to the pan. Heat, then add the onion, carrot, celery and bay leaf and cook over low heat for about 10 minutes, or until softened and golden. Add the garlic and wine, if using, increase the heat and boil for 3–4 minutes.

Add the stock and tomato and return the veal to the saucepan. Bring to the boil, then reduce the heat and simmer for 2½ hours, or until the meat is very tender.

Serve with mashed potato or steamed rice.

HINT: This recipe works with other less expensive cuts such as lamb forequarter pieces. If you are not using red wine, add an extra 250 ml (9 fl oz/1 cup) stock.

Kids of all ages run on snacks but never is it so important for the snacks to be healthy as when the kids are little. Think mini-meal and not plastic-wrapped convenience. Fresh and healthy means you will be ensuring good nutrition and good habits for their future. These snacks don't have to mean hours of preparation either; more often than not a well stocked fruit bowl or vegetable crisper is all that is needed.

simple snacks
& drinks

snack time

Little children need to eat little and often. Your toddler needs to eat at least five times a day, so the snacks you give her need to complement the other food she is eating.

With a little bit of planning when you shop you can have some simple, quick snacks on hand for those in-between times. You can also put some snacks into little storage pots or resealable plastic bags and use them in an emergency or when your child goes to kindergarten or childcare.

tips for healthy snacking:

• Offer snacks at regular times each day – just as is done at childcare. Make sure it is at least 1 hour before a meal.

• Serve snacks in the kitchen, or sit down together outside. Try not to serve them in front of the television.

• Aim for at least two different types of food in each snack. For example bread sticks and a piece of cheese, a muffin and a few grapes, or raw vegetables with a dip.

• Be a good role model. Don't eat something in front of your child that you would not give to her, for example a chocolate biscuit (cookie).

• Think creatively. You may have a piece of healthy home-made pizza left over from last night, or a hard-boiled egg in the refrigerator.

• Travel with snacks. When you go out always take at least two snacks and a drink with you. Pop them in an insulated bag for safe keeping.

• Include protein for an extra-satisfying snack. Cheese, peanut butter and egg are all good sources.

• Think about your child's teeth. Encourage your child to have a drink of water after a snack.

• Relax. If she occasionally has a packet of chips (crisps) or chocolate it's no big deal so long as they don't become an everyday thing.

vegetables with tzatziki dip

Snacks for toddlers don't need to be complicated, but they do need to be made from fresh healthy foods. This snack certainly fits the bill.

DIP

2 Lebanese (short) cucumbers, deseeded and grated

185 g (6½ oz/¾ cup) plain yoghurt

2 garlic cloves, crushed

1 teaspoon lemon juice

1 teaspoon chopped dill

½ teaspoon chopped mint

selection of sliced blanched vegetables (see Hints), to serve

Prep time: 15 minutes
Cooking time: Nil
Serves 4

Wrap the grated cucumber in a tea towel (dish towel) and squeeze out the excess water.

Mix the cucumber with the remaining ingredients and serve with the sliced vegetables. If you like, offer some poppadoms or chunks of bread.

HINTS: Choose your favourite vegetables or a selection which might include cauliflower, baby corn, broccoli, spring onion (scallion), beans, snow peas (mangetout), mushrooms, celery, zucchini (courgette), cucumber, capsicum (pepper), carrot and cherry tomatoes. Some vegetables (celery, cucumber, zucchini/courgette, carrot) will be extra crisp if refrigerated in a bowl of iced water before use. Other vegetables may soften if left in water.

sour cream dip

Combine 250 g (9 oz/1 cup) sour cream with ¼ teaspoon snipped dill, a pinch of sugar and 2 tablespoons thickened (whipping) cream. Pour into a small dish and place in the centre of a serving platter. Surround with a selection of blanched vegetables.

crunchy cheese bites

For healthy pastry snacks choose pastry that is made from good oils such as canola, olive or the polyunsaturated fats like sunflower or safflower. This makes these cheese bites a good snack for parents too.

250 g (9 oz/2 cups) grated cheddar cheese

125 g (4½ oz) feta cheese, crumbled

60 g (2¼ oz/¼ cup) ricotta cheese

30 g (1 oz/¼ cup) chopped spring onions (scallions)

1 small tomato, chopped

1 egg, beaten

4 sheets ready-rolled puff pastry

beaten egg, to brush

milk, to brush

Prep time: 15 minutes
Cooking time: 15 minutes
Makes about 20

Preheat the oven to 220°C (425°F/Gas 7). Combine the cheeses, spring onion, tomato and egg in a bowl. Season with freshly ground black pepper.

Cut the pastry into rounds using a 10 cm (4 inch) cutter. Place heaped teaspoons of the mixture onto one half of each round.

Fold the pastry over the filling to make semi-circles, brush the edges between the pastry with a little of the beaten egg and press the edges together firmly with a fork to seal.

Place on a baking tray and brush with a little milk. Bake in the oven for 10–15 minutes, or until puffed and golden. Allow the pastries to cool for at least 10 minutes before serving.

cheesy pinwheels

Alternatively, divide the cheese mixture from the recipe above into two and spread over 2 sheets of puff pastry, leaving a 1 cm (½ inch) border. Roll up firmly and trim the ends. Cut into 1.5 cm (⅝ inch) lengths and place on a lined baking tray. Bake for about 12–15 minutes, or until the pastry is puffed and golden. Cool for 5 minutes before removing from the tray, then serve warm. Makes 24.

pitta bread with hummus

Young toddlers will probably prefer to dip their fingers into the hummus. But as they get older, toddlers will enjoy dipping with pieces of pitta bread or vegetable sticks. Vegetable chips are also a great accompaniment to hummus.

220 g (7¾ oz/1 cup) dried chickpeas

80 ml (2½ fl oz/⅓ cup) olive oil

3–4 tablespoons lemon juice

2 garlic cloves, crushed

2 tablespoons tahini

1 tablespoon ground cumin

pitta bread, to serve

Prep time: 15 minutes + 8 hours soaking

Cooking time: 1 hour

Serves 4

Soak the chickpeas in water for 8 hours or overnight. Drain. Put in a saucepan, cover with cold water, bring to the boil and cook for around 50–60 minutes. Drain, reserving 185–250 ml (6–9 fl oz/¾–1 cup) of the cooking liquid.

Place the chickpeas in a food processor with the oil, lemon juice, garlic, tahini and cumin. Blend well until the mixture begins to look thick and creamy. With the motor running, gradually add the reserved cooking liquid until the mixture reaches the desired consistency. Serve with pitta bread, raw or blanched vegetables or vegetable chips (see below) or use as a spread for sandwiches.

vegetable chips

Preheat the oven to 180°C (350°F/Gas 4). Peel the skin of 500 g (1 lb 2 oz) each orange sweet potato, beetroot (beet) and parsnip. Run a vegetable peeler along the length of the sweet potato and beetroot to make thin ribbons. Cut the parsnip into thin slices. Fill a deep heavy-based saucepan one-third full of oil and heat to 190°C (375°F), or until a cube of bread dropped into the oil browns in 10 seconds. Cook the vegetables in batches for about 30 seconds, or until golden and crisp, turning with tongs if necessary. Drain on crumpled paper towels. Keep warm on a baking tray in the oven and cook the remaining chips (fries). Serve with the hummus.

muesli crunch biscuits

Because of their small tummies and high nutrition needs every food in a toddler's diet needs to count — including snacks. These biscuits hit the spot, combining the goodness of rolled oats and dried fruits.

125 g (4½ oz) unsalted butter

90 g (3¼ oz/½ cup) soft brown sugar

a few drops natural vanilla extract

1 egg

75 g (2¾ oz/½ cup) wholemeal (whole-wheat) self-raising flour

400 g (14 oz/3 cups) untoasted muesli (granola), without nuts

125 g (4½ oz/⅔ cup) chopped dried apricots

Prep time: 20 minutes
Cooking time: 15 minutes
Makes 24

Preheat the oven to 190°C (375°F/Gas 5). Lightly grease two large baking trays.

Cream the butter and sugar together, then add the vanilla and egg and beat well. Sift in the flour, add the muesli and stir in the chopped apricots. Shape the biscuit (cookie) mixture into balls, then place on the prepared trays and flatten lightly with a fork. Bake for about 10–12 minutes, or until lightly golden. Cool on a wire cooling rack, then store in an airtight container.

variation: Use corn-based cereal flakes or bran flakes instead of some of the muesli, and mix the chopped apricots with other dried fruits.

easy berry muffins

These delicious muffins couldn't be easier to make, so offer a great opportunity for eager toddlers to lend a hand in the kitchen.

250 g (9 oz/1 cup) plain yoghurt

100 g (3½ oz/1 cup) rolled (porridge) oats

60 ml (2 fl oz/¼ cup) oil

80 g (2¾ oz/⅓ cup) caster (superfine) sugar

1 egg

125 g (4½ oz/1 cup) self-raising flour, sifted

1C normal, 1tsp baking powder

3 teaspoons baking powder

300 g (10½ oz/1⅓ cups) mixed frozen berries, thawed

Prep time: 10 minutes
Cooking time: 25 minutes
Makes 16 muffins

Preheat the oven to 180°C (350°F/Gas 4). Place paper cases into 16 muffin holes. Mix together the yoghurt, oats, oil, caster sugar and egg. Gently stir in the sifted flour and baking powder with the fruit.

Spoon the mixture into paper cases in the muffin tin and bake for 20–25 minutes or until golden brown and a skewer comes out clean when inserted into the centre.

HINT: *Muffins can be made with any number of delicious fruit-based combinations. Aside from berry combinations, apple, sultanas (golden raisins) and cinnamon, or pear and date can make a tasty alternative.*

corn & ham muffins

Muffins are a good way to get extra fruit or vegies into your toddler's diet. Sweet corn is a good source of beta-carotene and B vitamins — especially niacin.

oil, for brushing

125 g (4½ oz/1 cup) self-raising flour

40 g (1½ oz/¼ cup) chopped ham

60 g (2¼ oz/⅓ cup) tinned corn kernels, drained

¼ red capsicum (pepper), deseeded and finely chopped

2 teapoons chopped parsley

60 g (2¼ oz) unsalted butter, melted

125 ml (4 fl oz/½ cup) milk

1 egg

1 tablespoon sesame seeds

Prep time: 10 minutes
Cooking time: 20 minutes
Makes 24

Preheat the oven to 210°C (415°C/Gas 6–7). Brush two 12-hole mini muffin tins with oil. Sift the flour into a large bowl. Add the ham, corn, capsicum and parsley and stir to combine.

In a small bowl, combine the melted butter, milk and egg. Make a well in the centre of the flour mixture and add the milk mixture. Mix the dough lightly with a fork or rubber spatula until the ingredients are just combined. (Do not overmix; the batter should be quite lumpy.)

Spoon the mixture into the prepared tins. Sprinkle the muffins with the sesame seeds. Bake the muffins for 15–20 minutes, or until golden. Cool on a wire rack.

variations: If you prefer, use wholemeal (whole-wheat) flour instead of white flour. A little extra milk may be required as wholemeal flour absorbs more liquid. Try adding other vegetables instead of the corn and capsicum, such as half a grated carrot and zucchini (courgette). For a vegetarian option, replace the ham with chopped, semi-dried (sun-blushed) tomatoes.

junior pikelets

A universal favourite, these carbohydrate-rich pikelets (griddle cakes) are bite-sized energy food for small children on the go.

125 g (4½ oz/1 cup) self-raising flour

¼ teaspoon bicarbonate of soda (baking soda)

2 tablespoons caster (superfine) sugar

125 ml (4 fl oz/½ cup) milk

1 egg

2 teaspoons oil, plus extra for greasing

60 g (2¼ oz/½ cup) sultanas (golden raisins)

Prep time: 10 minutes
Cooking time: 15 minutes
Makes 24

Sift the flour and bicarbonate of soda together into a bowl. Stir in the sugar. In a small bowl, combine the milk, egg and oil. Make a well in the centre and whisk in the milk mixture to make a smooth batter. Add the sultanas to the mixture and mix well.

Lightly grease and heat a frying pan with oil. Drop teaspoons of the batter into the pan and cook until bubbles form. Turn and cook the other side of the pikelet (griddle cake) until golden. Cool on a wire rack, then serve warm with butter. These pikelets be frozen, layered between sheets of baking paper, for up to 1 month.

banana smoothie

A nutritious drink like this is often all a toddler needs as a snack. Especially when made with bananas, which have twice the vitamin C of apples and pears.

1 banana

1 tablespoon plain yoghurt

1 teaspoon honey (optional, only for children over 12 months)

250 ml (9 fl oz/1 cup) milk

Prep time: 5 minutes

Cooking time: Nil

Serves 2

Peel the banana and roughly chop. Place in a blender with the yoghurt, honey, if using, and milk and blend until smooth, thick and creamy.

Pour into two glasses and serve.

HINT: The secret to the success of this smoothie is the preparation of the banana. The smoothie will be thicker and, as a result, more delicious if the banana is peeled and frozen for at least half an hour before it is used.

variation: Mangoes also work well in this smoothie, either as an accompaniment or added to the smoothie with the banana. Alternatively, you can add tinned peaches or apricots along with the banana for a delightful tangy taste.

vanilla milkshake

For the reluctant milk drinker there is nothing wrong with adding flavouring to encourage enjoyment. Research has shown that children who drink milk are often taller and have healthier bones and body weights than those who don't.

500 ml (17 fl oz/ 2 cups) milk, well chilled

1 teaspoon natural vanilla extract

sugar, to taste

Prep time: 5 minutes
Cooking time: Nil
Serves 2

Put the milk, vanilla extract and sugar into a large bowl or blender and whisk or blend for 20 seconds to combine.

Pour into two long cups and serve with straws for fun.

HINT: Milkshakes can be made using an electric blender, a whisk or a hand-held beater, or the ingredients can be placed in a tall sealed container and shaken until frothy.

variation: Your toddler's favourite fruit can be added to this recipe but it will need to be first processed in a blender to make it smooth.

berry froth

Berries are a good source of vitamin C and, for those with lots of seeds like raspberries, also a great source of fibre.

220 g (7¾ oz/1 cup) fresh or frozen mixed berries
500 ml (17 fl oz/2 cups) milk
2 ice cubes
sugar, to taste

Put the mixed berries, milk and ice cubes in a blender and blend until smooth. Add sugar and blend again until combined.

Pour into two long cups and serve with straws for fun.

Prep time: 5 minutes
Cooking time: Nil
Serves 2

fresh fruit slushy

This recipe for toddlers is a much healthier alternative to fruit juice as it has around four times the fibre of most commercial juices.

90 g (3¼ oz) fresh pineapple, peeled and cored
1 banana
3 kiwi fruit, sliced
250 ml (9 fl oz/1 cup) tropical fruit juice
2 ice cubes

Cut the pineapple and banana into chunks. Put in a blender with the kiwi fruit, fruit juice and ice cubes and blend until smooth.

Pour into four cups and serve.

Prep time: 10 minutes
Cooking time: Nil
Serves 4

Sweets are often a forbidden zone in the world of children's food. However, they don't necessarily deserve their bad reputation. Desserts aren't essential for young children but when you have time to prepare them, any of the fruit-based recipes in this chapter would complement a meal well. The recipes would also make a good snack but never use them as a bribe for the vegetables to be eaten!

something sweet

baked raisin apples

Tough, cooked skin will probably need to be removed for younger toddlers, but this fruit dessert makes a tasty and fibre-rich end to a meal.

4 cooking apples

80 g (2¾ oz/⅓ cup) soft brown sugar

1½ tablespoons chopped raisins

½ teaspoon ground cinnamon (optional)

20 g (¾ oz) unsalted butter

yoghurt or ricotta cream (see recipe below), to serve

Prep time: 10 minutes
Cooking time: 35 minutes
Serves 4

Preheat the oven to 220°C (425°F/Gas 7). Core the apples and score the skin around the middle. Combine the sugar, raisins and cinnamon. Place each apple on a piece of heavy-duty foil and stuff it with the filling. Spread a little butter over the top of each apple, then wrap the foil securely around the apples. Bake for about 35 minutes, or until cooked. Serve with yoghurt or ricotta cream.

HINT: These apples can also be baked on a covered barbecue.

ricotta cream

Whip equal quantities of ricotta cheese and Greek-style plain yoghurt together and sweeten slightly with soft brown sugar. You can use this as a dip for fresh or tinned fruits, as a creamy filling for pastries or in place of whipped cream.

bread & butter pudding

This is a wholesome sweet treat based upon bread, milk, eggs and fruit. It can be made even more nutritious if you use fibre-rich bread instead of white.

butter, for greasing

6 slices wholemeal (whole-wheat) bread

750 ml (26 fl oz/3 cups) milk

¼ teaspoon grated lemon zest

110 g (3¾ oz/½ cup) sugar

4 eggs

125 g (4½ oz/¾ cup) mixed dried fruits (sultanas/golden raisins, raisins, chopped dried apricots, currants, mixed peel/ mixed candied citrus peel)

Prep time: 20 minutes + 10 minutes standing

Cooking time: 35 minutes

Serves 4

Preheat the oven to 180°C (350°F/Gas 4). Grease an ovenproof dish. Remove the crusts and thickly butter the bread.

Heat the milk in a saucepan and add the lemon zest. Bring to the boil, then cover and remove from the heat, leaving to infuse for 10 minutes. Beat the sugar and eggs together, then strain the milk over the eggs and mix well.

Scatter half the dried fruit over the bottom of the prepared dish and arrange the bread, buttered sides down, on top. Pour in half the custard, then repeat with the remaining fruit, bread and custard. Place the dish in a baking tin and add enough water to fill halfway up the outside of the dish. Bake for 35 minutes.

apple sago pudding

Sago is made from the dried starchy granules found in the pith of Indonesian palm trees. Its unique texture will likely spark the interest of young eaters.

80 g (2¾ oz/⅓ cup) caster (superfine) sugar

100 g (3½ oz/½ cup) sago

600 ml (21 fl oz) milk

40 g (1½ oz/⅓ cup) sultanas (golden raisins)

1 teaspoon natural vanilla extract

pinch of ground nutmeg

¼ teaspoon ground cinnamon

2 eggs, lightly beaten

3 small ripe apples (about 250 g/9 oz), peeled, cored and very thinly sliced

1 tablespoon soft brown sugar

Prep time: 15 minutes
Cooking time: 50 minutes
Serves 4

Preheat the oven to 180°C (350°F/Gas 4). Grease a 1.5 litre (52 fl oz/6 cup) ceramic soufflé dish. Place the sugar, sago, milk and sultanas in a saucepan. Heat the mixture, stirring often. Bring to the boil, then reduce the heat and simmer for 5 minutes.

Stir in the vanilla extract, nutmeg, cinnamon, egg and the apple slices, then pour into the prepared dish. Sprinkle with the brown sugar and bake for 45 minutes, or until set and golden brown.

choc-banana bites

Besides being a good source of vitamin C and energy-giving carbohydrates, bananas are a great easy-to-handle fruit for kids.

5 wooden iceblock
(popsicle/ice lolly) sticks, cut
in half

3 large bananas, peeled and
cut into 3 pieces

125 g (4½ oz) dark cooking
chocolate, chopped

Prep time: 10 minutes +
4 hours freezing

Cooking time: 5 minutes

Makes 9

Line a 33 x 28 cm (13 x 11¼ inch) baking tray with foil. Carefully push a half-stick into each piece of banana. Place on the prepared tray and freeze for 2 hours or until firm.

Put the chocolate in a small heatproof bowl. Stand the bowl over a saucepan of simmering water and stir until the chocolate has melted and is smooth.

Working with one banana piece at a time, dip each piece into the hot chocolate mixture, turning to fully coat. Drain off any excess chocolate. Place the banana pieces on the prepared tray. Refrigerate until the chocolate has set, then wrap in plastic wrap and place in the freezer for at least 2 hours to harden. Serve frozen.

frozen fruit yoghurt

This sweet snack is a good source of calcium and fibre — try freezing some into iceblock (popsicle/ice lolly) moulds for healthy treats on hot days.

60 g (2¼ oz/½ cup) fresh fruit salad (pineapple, apple, banana, peach, apricot, orange)

125 g (4½ oz/½ cup) plain yoghurt

Prep time: 5 minutes + 4 hours freezing

Cooking time: Nil

Serves 2

Put the fruit salad in a blender, add the yoghurt and purée. Pour the mixture into a freezer tray and freeze.

For a lighter texture, remove the mixture from the freezer, return to the blender and whip, then refreeze. Repeat once more.

strawberry parfait

Jelly and ice cream — what more could a child want, except perhaps some strawberries! This is a sweet that is perfect for an occasional extra.

85 g (3 oz) strawberry-flavoured jelly crystals (gelatine dessert)

250 g (9 oz) strawberries, hulled

500 g (1 lb 2 oz) vanilla ice cream

Prep time: 10 minutes + setting time

Cooking time: Nil

Serves 6

Put the jelly crystals (gelatine dessert) in a heatproof bowl and pour over 250 ml (9 fl oz/1 cup) boiling water. Stir to dissolve the crystals, then add 250 ml (9 fl oz/1 cup) cold water. Refrigerate until set.

Process half the strawberries in a food processor until smooth. Reserve the remaining strawberries to top the parfait.

Spoon the jelly evenly between six cups. Top the jelly with the puréed strawberries and the ice cream. Finally, add the reserved strawberries and serve immediately.

HINT: Halve the strawberries if they are large.

frozen fruit kebabs

New and unusual ways to eat fruit will always appeal to a curious toddler, so these fruit kebabs should be a hit!

140 g (5 oz) fresh pineapple

½ mango

80 g (2¾ oz) fresh seedless watermelon

100 g (3½ oz) fresh rockmelon or any orange-fleshed melon

4 iceblock (popsicle/ice lolly) sticks

Prep time: 10 minutes + 4 hours freezing

Cooking time: Nil

Makes 4

Remove the skin from all the fruit and cut each type into four cubes. Thread onto the iceblock sticks and freeze for 4 hours or until frozen. To serve, remove from the freezer 10 minutes before eating to allow them to soften slightly.

HINT: Extra quantities of this recipe can be made and kept in the freezer for a hot day.

Celebrating doesn't have to mean unhealthy food, as you will find out in this chapter. Foods with crunch, colour and sweetness can all be tasty and good for your child too! Of course there will always be foods that are purely for the joy of the occasion but when the party is on, you will want to know that some of what they are eating is going to count as nutritious!

birthdays & other occasions

chicken nuggets

These nuggets are a tasty, high-protein, low-salt party food that will be as big a hit as their unhealthy fast-food counterparts.

melted butter, for greasing

375 g (13 oz) boneless, skinless chicken thighs, roughly chopped

1 egg

1 tablespoon snipped fresh chives

¼ teaspoon sesame oil

2 teaspoons plum sauce

1 teaspoon salt-reduced soy sauce

30 g (1 oz/1 cup) corn-based cereal flakes

Prep time: 20 minutes
Cooking time: 15 minutes
Makes 34

Preheat the oven to 180°C (350°F/Gas 4). Line a 33 x 28 cm (13 x 11¼ in) baking tray with foil. Brush with melted butter or oil.

Put the chicken, egg, chives, sesame oil and sauces in a food processor. Process for 30 seconds, or until the mixture is smooth.

Shape heaped teaspoons of the mixture into balls. Roll the balls in the corn-based cereal flakes. Place the nuggets on the prepared tray. Bake for 15 minutes, or until golden and crisp.

cheese & bacon tarts

These yummy little tarts are rich with the goodness of cheese and egg and if you choose a shortcrust (pie) pastry made with healthy fats (canola or sunflower oils), then birthday treats are as healthy as they can be.

melted butter, for greasing

2 sheets ready-rolled shortcrust (pie) pastry

2 slices bacon, finely chopped

1 small onion, finely chopped

125 ml (4 fl oz/½ cup) cream (whipping)

1 egg

½ teaspoon mild mustard

60 g (2¼ oz/½ cup) grated cheddar cheese

Prep time: 30 minutes
Cooking time: 15 minutes
Makes 18

Preheat the oven to 180°C (350°F/Gas 4). Brush two 12-hole mini muffin tins with melted butter.

Lay out the pastry on a lightly floured work surface. Cut out rounds with a 7 cm (2¾ inch) fluted cutter. Ease the pastry rounds into the muffin holes. Sprinkle the chopped bacon and onion over the pastry shells. Combine the cream, egg and mustard in a small bowl and whisk until smooth. Spoon 1 teaspoon of the mixture into each pastry case. Sprinkle with the grated cheese. Bake the tarts for 15 minutes, or until golden and crisp. Serve warm.

variation: If you like, you can substitute drained and flaked tinned salmon for the chopped bacon.

sausage rolls

Prepared ahead and frozen, home-made sausage rolls are as convenient as ready-made ones while having the benefit of being lower in salt and fat.

1 teaspoon oil, plus extra, for greasing

1 onion, finely chopped

500 g (1 lb 2 oz) sausage mince (meat)

80 g (2¾ oz/1 cup) soft white breadcrumbs

2 tablespoons tomato sauce (ketchup)

1 egg, lightly beaten

2 sheets frozen ready-rolled puff pastry, thawed

beaten egg or milk, for glazing

Prep time: 35 minutes
Cooking time: 30 minutes
Makes 48

Preheat the oven to 210°C (415°F/Gas 6–7). Lightly grease a baking tray with oil.

Heat the oil in a frying pan. Add the onion and cook, over low heat, for 2–3 minutes, or until soft and transparent. Put the onion, meat, breadcrumbs, tomato sauce and egg into a bowl and mix together.

Lay the pastry sheets on a lightly floured work surface and cut into three horizontal strips. Divide the meat mixture into six equal portions and place across the long edge of the pastry. Roll the pastry up to form long sausage shapes. Brush lightly with a little beaten egg or milk. Cut the rolls into 4 cm (1½ inch) lengths and place on the prepared tray.

Bake for 10 minutes, then reduce the heat to 180°C (350°F/Gas 4) and bake for a further 15 minutes, or until golden.

HINT: These sausage rolls can be frozen for up to 2 weeks before serving. Thaw and reheat them in a 180°C (350°F/Gas 4) oven for around 15–20 minutes, or until hot.

baby burgers

These mini burgers will best suit older toddlers who will be more able to hold and eat them than younger children. However, that doesn't mean that they won't enjoy dissecting them and eating each piece separately!

500 g (1 lb 2 oz) minced (ground) beef

1 small onion, finely chopped

1 tablespoon finely chopped flat-leaf (Italian) parsley

1 egg, lightly beaten

1 tablespoon tomato sauce (ketchup)

2 tablespoons oil

½ lettuce, finely shredded

2 small tomatoes, thinly sliced

10 small bread rolls, halved

5 cheese slices, halved

5 tinned pineapple rings, drained and halved

tomato sauce (ketchup) or barbecue sauce

Prep time: 30 minutes
Cooking time: 10 minutes
Makes 10

Combine the beef, onion, parsley, beaten egg and tomato sauce in a large bowl. Using your hands, mix until well combined. Divide the mixture into 10 portions. Shape into round patties.

Heat the oil in a large, heavy-based pan over medium heat. Cook the patties for 5 minutes on each side, or until they are well browned and cooked through. Remove and drain on paper towels.

To assemble the burger, put the lettuce and tomato on the base of the roll. Top with the meat patty, cheese slice and pineapple slice. Add the sauce and cover with the remaining roll half. Serve immediately.

vegie puffs

These tasty pastries look just like sausage rolls except they are packed with the goodness of vegetables and cheese. Serve them with tomato sauce (ketchup).

I small potato, diced

I small carrot, diced

I zucchini (courgette), diced

I celery stalk, diced

40 g (1½ oz/¼ cup) diced pumpkin (winter squash)

15 g (½ oz/¼ cup) chopped broccoli

15 g (½ oz/¼ cup) chopped cauliflower

250 g (9 oz/2 cups) grated cheddar cheese

I sheet frozen, ready-rolled puff pastry, halved

milk, for the pastry

Prep time: 15 minutes

Cooking time: 15 minutes

Makes 12

Put the vegetables in a small saucepan and add enough water to cover. Bring to the boil, then reduce the heat and simmer for 3 minutes. Drain well and transfer the vegetables to a bowl to cool. Add the cheese and mix well.

Preheat the oven to 220°C (425°F/Gas 7). Lay the two pieces of pastry on a work surface, divide the mixture in half and spread it along the long side of each piece.

Roll up the pastry to form a sausage shape, brush the edge with a little milk and press to seal.

Cut each roll into six even-sized pieces. Make a small slit in the centre of each and place on a lightly greased baking tray. Brush with milk and bake for 10 minutes, or until crisp and golden.

HINT: These can be made ahead of time and frozen before cooking. To cook, thaw and follow the recipe above.

money bags

These little parcels are a fun, easy-to-hold food with a great crunch factor. This recipe also gives you the option of a making them more exotic by using Asian flavourings (don't forget that this will add more salt).

1 tablespoon peanut oil

4 spring onions (scallions), finely chopped

2 garlic cloves, crushed

1 tablespoon grated fresh ginger

150 g (5½ oz) minced (ground) chicken

150 g (5½ oz) minced (ground) pork

2 teaspoons salt-reduced soy sauce

2 teaspoons soft brown sugar

2 teaspoons lime juice (optional)

2 teaspoons fish sauce (optional)

3 tablespoons finely chopped coriander (cilantro) leaves

30 won ton wrappers

oil, for deep-frying

garlic chives, for tying

Prep time: 30 minutes + cooling time
Cooking time: 15 minutes
Makes 30

Heat a wok over medium heat, add the oil and swirl to coat. Add the spring onions, garlic and ginger and cook for 1–2 minutes, or until the onions are soft. Add the meats and cook for 4 minutes, or until cooked, breaking up the lumps.

Stir in the soy sauce, brown sugar, lime juice and fish sauce, if using, and coriander. Cook, stirring, for 1–2 minutes, or until mixed and dry. Set aside to cool.

Place 2 teaspoons of filling in the centre of each won ton wrapper, then lightly brush the edges with water. Lift the sides up tightly and pinch around the filling to form a bag. Trim the edges if necessary.

Fill a clean wok one-third full of oil and heat to 190°C (375°F), or until a cube of bread dropped in the oil browns in 10 seconds. Cook in batches for 30–60 seconds, or until golden and crisp. Drain on crumpled paper towels, then tie with the chives to serve.

three cheese & chicken pizza

Time is often of the essence on party day. For a quicker version of this recipe buy a pre-prepared pizza base from your bakery or supermarket.

BASE

250 g (9 oz/2 cups) self-raising flour

30 g (1 oz) unsalted butter, chopped

80 ml (2½ fl oz/⅓ cup) milk

80 ml (2½ fl oz/⅓ cup) water

TOPPING

100 g (3½ oz/⅓ cup) spreadable feta cheese

100 g (3½ oz/⅓ cup) ricotta cheese

1 tablespoon finely chopped basil

½ barbecued (grilled) chicken, skin and bones discarded (see Hints)

80 g (2¾ oz/½ cup) semi-dried (sun-blushed) tomatoes, finely chopped

4 balls bocconcini (baby mozzarella cheese) (about 60 g/2¼ oz each), thinly sliced

Prep time: 15 minutes
Cooking time: 25 minutes
Serves 4

Preheat the oven to 220°C (425°F/Gas 7). Lightly grease a 30 cm (12 inch) round pizza tray with oil.

To make the base, put the flour in a bowl and use your fingertips to rub in the butter until it looks like breadcrumbs. Make a well in the centre and pour in enough of the combined milk and water to mix to a soft dough. Turn out onto a lightly floured work surface and knead lightly to form a ball. Roll out to a 30 cm (12 inch) circle and place on the prepared tray.

To make the topping, combine the feta, ricotta and basil and spread over the pizza base leaving a 1 cm (½ inch) border. Chop the chicken into small pieces and sprinkle over the pizza with the tomato. Cover with the bocconcini slices and bake for 20–25 minutes, or until the base is golden and cooked through and the cheese is melted. Cut into wedges and serve.

HINTS: Half a barbecued (grilled) chicken gives about 185 g (6½ oz) chicken meat or 1¼ cups finely chopped meat. If bocconcini is unavailable, you can use mozzarella.

fish cocktails

Just because it's good for you doesn't mean it can't be party food. Toddlers will get a healthy serve of brain food from these nuggets and enjoy their crunchiness.

250 g (9 oz) boneless white fish fillets

2 tablespoons plain (all-purpose) flour

1 egg white

15 g (½ oz/¼ cup) crushed corn-based cereal flakes

mayonnaise, to serve

Prep time: 20 minutes
Cooking time: 15 minutes
Makes 24

Preheat the oven to 180°C (350°F/Gas 4). Cut the fish into 3 cm (1¼ inch) cubes. Coat the fish pieces in flour and shake off any excess.

Whisk the egg white in a small bowl. Dip the fish, one cube at a time, in the egg white, then coat with the crushed cereal flakes. Place in a single layer on a baking tray. Bake for 15 minutes, or until golden, turning the pieces over after 10 minutes. Serve hot with mayonnaise or your toddler's favourite seafood sauce.

oven chips

Children just love chips (fries) and potatoes are chock full of carbohydrates — just what toddlers need to give them the energy they need for party games.

6 medium potatoes
60 ml (2 fl oz/¼ cup) olive oil

Prep time: 10 minutes
Cooking time: 45 minutes
Serves 6

Preheat the oven to 220°C (425°F/Gas 7). Peel the potatoes, and cut them into slices about 1 cm (½ inch) square.

Soak the chips (fries) in cold water for 10 minutes. Drain well, then pat dry thoroughly with paper towels.

Spread the chips onto a baking tray and sprinkle the oil over them. Toss them to coat well. Bake the chips for 45 minutes until golden and crisp, turning occasionally.

choc-chip crackles

These crunchy chocolate treats filled with sultanas (golden raisins) and choc chips will be full of surprises for small party goers.

90 g (3¼ oz/3 cups) puffed rice cereal

30 g (1 oz/¼ cup) unsweetened cocoa powder

150 g (5½ oz/1¼ cups) icing (confectioners') sugar

60 g (2¼ oz/½ cup) sultanas (golden raisins)

60 g (2¼ oz/⅔ cup) desiccated coconut

200 g (7 oz) Copha (white vegetable shortening), melted

60 g (2¼ oz/⅓ cup) dark choc chips

Prep time: 20 minutes
Cooking time: 5 minutes
Makes 24

Line two 12-hole mini muffin tins with foil cases. Combine the puffed rice cereal, cocoa and sugar in a large bowl. Mix thoroughly, then stir in the sultanas and coconut. Stir in the melted shortening.

Spoon the mixture into the prepared muffin tins. Sprinkle with the choc chips. Refrigerate until set.

martian biscuits

For any chemical-sensitive party goers, ice a set of biscuits (cookies) as 'snowmen' without the green colouring. This way no one will miss out.

125 g (4½ oz) unsalted butter

115 g (4 oz/½ cup) caster (superfine) sugar

1 egg

210 g (7½ oz/1¾ cups) plain (all-purpose) flour

125 g (4½ oz/1 cup) icing (confectioners') sugar

60 ml (2 fl oz/¼ cup) hot water

4 drops green food colouring

1 packet liquorice allsorts, thinly sliced

Prep time: 20 minutes + 30 minutes refrigeration

Cooking time: 15 minutes

Makes 10

To make the biscuits (cookies), beat the butter, sugar and egg using electric beaters in a medium bowl until light and creamy.

Add the flour to the mixture. Using your hands, press the mixture together to form a soft dough. Turn onto a lightly floured work surface and knead for 2 minutes, or until smooth. Refrigerate, covered with plastic wrap, for 30 minutes.

Preheat the oven to 180°C (350°F/Gas 4). Brush a 33 × 28 cm (13 × 11¼ inch) baking tray with melted butter or oil. Roll the dough, between sheets of baking paper, to 5 mm (¼ inch) thickness. Cut into shapes using a 12 cm (4½ inch) people-shaped biscuit (cookie) cutter. Place on the prepared tray and bake for 15 minutes, or until golden. Leave to cool on a wire rack.

Place the sifted icing sugar in a medium bowl. Add the water and food colouring and stir until well combined. Dip the front of each biscuit into the icing (frosting), holding the biscuits over the bowl to allow any excess icing to drain away. While the icing is still soft, decorate the biscuits with liquorice allsorts. The biscuits can be made up to 7 days ahead and stored in an airtight container.

gingerbread people

If you can handle the 'help' when making your gingerbread characters, offer a small amount of dough to your toddler and let him roll and cut his own shapes.

125 g (4½ oz) unsalted butter

90 g (3¼ oz/½ cup) soft brown sugar

115 g (4 oz/⅓ cup) golden syrup (dark corn syrup)

1 egg

250 g (9 oz/2 cups) plain (all-purpose) flour

40 g (1½ oz/⅓ cup) self-raising flour

1 tablespoon ground ginger

1 teaspoon bicarbonate of soda (baking soda)

ICING

1 egg white

½ teaspoon lemon juice

125 g (4½ oz/1 cup) icing (confectioners') sugar

food colourings

Prep time: 30 minutes + 15 minutes refrigeration

Cooking time: 15 minutes

Makes 15–20, depending on size of cutters

Line two or three baking trays with baking paper. Using electric beaters, beat the butter, sugar and syrup in a large bowl until light and creamy. Add the egg and beat well.

Sift in the flours, ginger and bicarbonate of soda. Use a knife to mix until just combined.

Use a well-floured hand to gather the dough into a ball. Knead gently on a well-floured surface until smooth. Don't over-handle the dough or it will become tough.

Lay a sheet of baking paper over a large chopping board. Roll out the dough on the lined board to a 5 mm (¼ inch) thickness. Preheat the oven to 180°C (350°F/Gas 4).

Refrigerate the dough on the board for 15 minutes, or until it is firm enough to cut. Cut the dough into shapes using assorted gingerbread people cutters. Press any remaining dough together. Re-roll and cut out into shapes.

Bake for 10–12 minutes, or until lightly browned. Cool the biscuits on the trays, then decorate with the icing (frosting).

To make the icing, beat the egg white in a small bowl with electric beaters until soft peaks form. Gradually add the lemon juice and sifted icing sugar and beat until thick and creamy.

Divide the icing into several bowls and tint with food colourings. Spoon into small paper icing bags and use to decorate the biscuits.

butterfly cupcakes

Not many toddlers can resist helping out when it comes to baking. Let them put the paper cases into the muffin tin, help pour measured ingredients into the mixing bowl and, of course, lick the beaters when it is all done!

125 g (4½ oz) unsalted butter, softened

170 g (6 oz/¾ cup) caster (superfine) sugar

185 g (6½ oz/1½ cups) self-raising flour

125 ml (4 fl oz/½ cup) milk

2 eggs

125 ml (4 fl oz/½ cup) thickened (whipping) cream

1½ tablespoons strawberry jam

icing (confectioners') sugar, to dust

Prep time: 10 minutes
Cooking time: 20 minutes
Makes 18

Preheat the oven to 180°C (350°F/Gas 4). Line 18 holes in two muffin tins with paper cases. Beat the butter, sugar, flour, milk and eggs with electric beaters on low speed. Increase the speed and beat until smooth and pale. Divide the mixture evenly among the cases and bake for 30 minutes, or until cooked and golden. Transfer to a wire rack to cool.

Cut shallow rounds from the centre of each cake using the point of a sharp knife, then cut the rounds in half. Spoon 2 teaspoons cream into each cavity, top with 1 teaspoon jam and position two halves of the cake tops in the jam to resemble butterfly wings. Dust with icing sugar.

Alternatively, do not cut out the centre of the cake and cover each cupcake with buttercream or chocolate buttercream (see below).

buttercream

With electric beaters, beat 125 g (4½ oz) unsalted butter until pale and fluffy. Continue beating and gradually add 1 teaspoon natural vanilla extract and 185 g (6½ oz/1½ cups) sifted icing (confectioners') sugar. Gradually add 2 tablespoons milk, at room temperature. Beat the mixture until smooth.

chocolate buttercream

To make chocolate buttercream, mix 2 tablespoons sifted unsweetened cocoa powder into the above mixture.

teddy birthday cake

A good old-fashioned butter cake makes good sense as a birthday cake for toddlers — particularly when made into a teddy bear.

445 g (15¾ oz) unsalted butter, softened

350 g (12 oz/1½ cups) caster (superfine) sugar

1 tablespoon natural vanilla extract

6 eggs, lightly beaten

550 g (1 lb 4 oz/4⅓ cups) self-raising flour

250 ml (9 fl oz/1 cup) milk

1½ quantities buttercream, from recipe on page 195

30 g (1 oz/¼ cup) unsweetened cocoa powder

DECORATION

five 5 cm (2 inch) jam rollettes (mini jelly rolls)

2 round chocolate biscuits (cookies)

2 milk chocolate drops

1 white marshmallow, halved

liquorice pieces

1 red jellybean

Prep time: 1 hour
Cooking time: 35–40 minutes
Makes 1 cake

Preheat the oven to 180°C (350°F/Gas 4). Grease and line the bases of two 18 cm (7 inch) round cake tins and a 1 litre (35 fl oz/4 cup) basin.

To make the cake, beat the butter and sugar until light and creamy. Add the vanilla extract and eggs one at a time, beating well after each addition. Fold in the sifted flour alternately with the milk until smooth.

Divide the cake mix evenly among the three tins and bake for 35–40 minutes, or until a skewer inserted into the centre comes out clean. Cool for 5 minutes, then turn out onto a wire rack to cool.

Spread the top of one round cake with some buttercream. Sandwich the round cakes together. Cut away the top and bottom edges of the cake sandwich to form a slight ball shape. This will be the fat body. Sit the pudding-shaped cake on top. Secure with skewers. Trim a diagonal slice around the bottom edge of the pudding for a neck.

Cut a diagonal slice off the end of four rollettes and attach them to the body with skewers to form the arms and legs. Cut a slice off the remaining rollette and attach it to the centre of the face with a skewer to form the snout. For ears, make two slits on the top of each side of the head then push a round biscuit (cookie) into each.

Put 4 tablespoons of the buttercream in a bowl. Add the cocoa to the remainder and beat well. With a palette knife, spread the chocolate icing over the body, arms and legs (reserving a tablespoon for piping). Ice the tummy, snout and ears with the white buttercream.

For the eyes, stick a chocolate drop on each marshmallow half with icing. Use liquorice for the lips and nose and a jellybean for the mouth. Ice paw marks on the arms and legs with reserved chocolate icing.

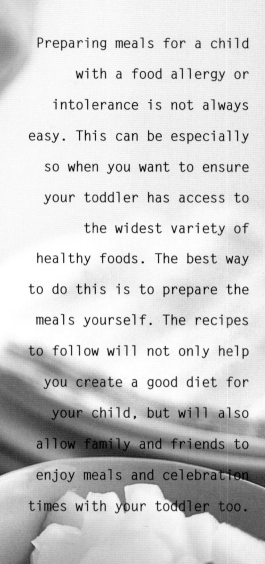

Preparing meals for a child with a food allergy or intolerance is not always easy. This can be especially so when you want to ensure your toddler has access to the widest variety of healthy foods. The best way to do this is to prepare the meals yourself. The recipes to follow will not only help you create a good diet for your child, but will also allow family and friends to enjoy meals and celebration times with your toddler too.

food allergy &
intolerance

problems with food

FOODS MOST LIKELY
TO CAUSE AN ALLERGIC
REACTION IN CHILDREN:

- *Eggs*

- *Cow's milk*

- *Peanuts and other nuts*

- *Soy*

- *Wheat*

- *Fish*

FOOD ADDITIVES MOST
LIKELY TO CAUSE AN
ADVERSE REACTION:

- *Colours: 102, 107, 110,
122–129, 132, 133, 142, 151,
155, 160B (natural)*

- *Preservatives: 200–203,
210–218, 220–228,
249–252, 280–283,
310–312, 319–321*

- *Flavour enhancers:
620–635, hydrolyzed
vegetable protein (HVP),
textured vegetable
protein (TVP)*

In cases of unexplained problems, a food allergy is often the first to be blamed, but the diagnosis of allergies is a highly scientific exercise and real allergic reactions to food are not as common as many believe. Food allergy is in fact quite rare; most reactions to food are a food intolerance.

A food allergy is an abnormal reaction by the body's defence system to proteins found in food. One of the defining characteristics of food allergy is the almost instantaneous symptoms that can occur when the offending food is eaten. Foods most likely to cause an allergic reaction (see box left) are not usually introduced to babies as first foods for this very reason.

Babies from allergic families are at a higher risk of developing a food allergy than those who are not. For this reason it is recommended that the introduction of these foods into the diet of these babies be delayed by several months or more than the usual introduction times. A dietitian should be consulted for more detailed information about this.

The symptoms of food allergy in young children include swelling (particularly around the mouth), hives, rashes and eczema. Less common is diarrhoea, vomiting, wheezing or asthma. Severe allergies can result in the potentially fatal state of hyperreactivity known as anaphylaxis.

The good news for allergic children is that most will outgrow their food allergy by the time they go to school. The allergies most likely not to disappear are those to peanuts, or other nuts, and fish — these tend to be lifelong.

There may be many other causes of the types of symptoms seen in food allergies, so it is recommended that you seek expert help before changing your child's diet. Treatment of a true food allergy requires complete exclusion of the food or food group from the diet. For young children in particular this needs the specialized help of a dietitian to make sure their diet is adequate for their growth and development.

food intolerance

Food intolerances are reactions to the chemicals found in food — both natural and added. These reactions, unlike a food allergy, are not a response by the immune system but are instead thought to be the result of irritation to nerve endings. Unlike an allergy, the symptoms of food intolerance are rarely associated with the food most recently consumed. Symptoms of food intolerance come about when tolerance thresholds for 'culprit chemicals' are reached. As such they may occur many hours after eating the offending food(s).

Foods likely to cause intolerance in sensitive children are those rich in the natural chemicals salicylate, amine and glutamate. The list of these foods is quite extensive so it is easier to consider those which are least likely to cause a problem (see box right) than those which are problematic. As with the case of an allergy, many of these 'lower chemical' foods are given as first foods, with the higher chemical foods being introduced a little later.

Added chemicals (see box opposite) can also be problematic for some children, occasionally resulting in emotional and behavioural symptoms. Because foods containing added chemicals don't feature highly in the diets of babies or younger toddlers, they are more likely to be an issue in 3 and 4 year-olds.

Food intolerance symptoms are wide ranging and include those symptoms seen in food allergies such as rashes, eczema and hives as well as colic, diarrhoea, nappy rash, vomiting and general irritability. Once again, because these symptoms could have many other causes than food, it is important to have your child seen by an expert before restricting their diet. Treatment of food intolerances is complex and may require complete or only partial elimination of high problem foods from the diet. A dietitian specializing in food allergy and intolerance is best qualified to give you this advice.

FOODS LEAST LIKELY TO BE IMPLICATED IN FOOD INTOLERANCE:

- *Vegetables — brussels sprouts, cabbage (green and red), celery, chives, choko/chayote, dried peas, beans and lentils, leeks, iceberg lettuce, potato, swede/ rutabaga, shallots, parsley*

- *Fruit — pear*

- *Cereals — rice, barley, sago, soy, rye, wheat, buckwheat, cornflour/cornstarch*

- *Fats and oils — butter, margarine (unpreserved, no antioxidant), safflower, sunflower, canola and soy oils*

- *Protein foods — beef, chicken, eggs, fish, lamb, veal*

- *Drinks — cow's milk, soy beverage, lemonade (unpreserved), rice beverage*

lactose intolerance

The natural sugar in all kinds of milk is known as lactose, and is an important source of energy for babies. Lactase is the enzyme in the digestive system that helps to break down the lactose in milk. When not enough of this enzyme is present the digestive system cannot cope and lactose intolerance results.

The most common symptoms of lactose intolerance are bloating, tummy pain and diarrhoea. These symptoms can be caused by other conditions so it is important to seek advice to confirm that this is the problem. In babies and young children, lactose intolerance is not common except as a result of gastroenteritis and other diarrhoea-causing illnesses. This type of lactose intolerance is only temporary, but formula-fed babies should be fed a lactose-free formula for a few weeks. Breast-fed babies should continue to be breast-fed. With toddlers, the removal of high-lactose foods like milk, yoghurt and ice cream is usually recommended. Calcium-enriched soy beverages and processed cheddar can continue to provide much needed calcium until the intolerance resolves itself.

buckwheat pancakes

Contrary to its name, buckwheat is not related to wheat at all and so, unlike wheat, is a gluten-free grain. Free of egg, dairy, gluten, nut and soy.

130 g (4¾ oz/1 cup)
buckwheat flour

1 egg, or equivalent
egg replacer

185 ml (6 fl oz/¾ cup) water

canola oil, for greasing

125 ml (4 fl oz/½ cup)
maple syrup

Prep time: 10 minutes
Cooking time: 20 minutes
Makes 16–20 pancakes

Sift the flour into a bowl and make a well in the centre. Add the combined egg or egg replacer and water. Beat with a wooden spoon until well combined and smooth. Pour the batter into a vessel with a pouring lip.

Brush a 20 cm (8 inch) frying pan with oil and heat over medium heat. Pour in just enough batter to thinly cover the bottom of the pan. When the top of the pancake starts to set, turn it over with a spatula and cook for a further 30 seconds. Transfer to a plate. Repeat with the remaining pancake batter, greasing the pan between batches. Serve with a drizzle of maple syrup.

rolled rice porridge

Rice is an important source of energy-giving carbohydrate ideal for small food-sensitive tummies. Free of egg, dairy, gluten, nut and soy.

50 g (1¾ oz/½ cup) rolled rice or rice flakes

golden syrup or maple syrup, to serve

peeled and chopped pear, to serve

pear juice (see page 234), to serve

Prep time: 5 minutes
Cooking time: 20 minutes
Serves 4

Combine the rolled rice or rice flakes and 500 ml (17 fl oz/2 cups) boiling water in a saucepan. Cover with a lid and simmer over medium heat for 20 minutes, or until soft and creamy. Serve topped with golden or maple syrup, chopped pear and pear juice.

HINT: If you'd like a sweeter porridge, try adding a little pear juice in place of the water. You'll need to bring it to the boil before using it.

creamy rice porridge

Free of egg, dairy, gluten, nut and soy.

For a deliciously creamy taste, make the porridge with a non-dairy alternative, such as rice drink. Bring 500 ml (17 fl oz/2 cups) rice drink to the boil in a saucepan, then proceed with the recipe.

potato & leek fritters

If citrus fruits are off the menu, then potatoes become a good alternative source of vitamin C for your toddler. This recipe has more than their daily needs in one serve. Free of egg, dairy, gluten, nut and soy.

1.25 kg (2 lb 12 oz) white-skinned potatoes

1 leek, washed

2 eggs, lightly beaten, or equivalent egg replacer

1 tablespoon rice flour

2 tablespoons canola oil

Prep time: 15 minutes
Cooking time: 20 minutes
Serves 4–6

Peel and grate the potatoes. Pat the potato dry and put in a bowl. Finely chop the white part of the leek and add it to the bowl with the potato. Add the eggs or egg replacer and rice flour. Mix until combined.

Heat the oil in a large non-stick frying pan. Drop tablespoons of the mixture into the pan — you may need to cook the fritters in batches. Fry on each side for a few minutes, or until golden brown. Serve hot or cold either on their own or with baked beans.

HINTS: Use plain brushed potatoes. Red-skinned and new potatoes have moderate levels of natural flavour substances. Peeled potato will discolour if left to stand for too long.

chickpea dip

Legumes such as chickpeas are a 'low chemical' source of vegetable protein plus iron and the B vitamin folic acid. Free of egg, dairy, gluten, nut and soy.

125 g (4½ oz) tinned chickpeas, rinsed and drained (see Hints)

¼ teaspoon citric acid (see Hints)

60 ml (2 fl oz/¼ cup) pear juice (see page 234)

2 garlic cloves, crushed

2 tablespoons canola oil

Prep time: 15 minutes

Cooking time: Nil

Makes 250 g (9 oz/1 cup)

Combine the chickpeas, citric acid, pear juice, garlic, oil and 2 tablespoons water in a food processor. Process until smooth — the mixture should be the consistency of thick mayonnaise.

Scoop into a bowl and serve with crispy wafer biscuits (see the recipe opposite), chilled sticks of soft or blanched vegetables such as celery or carrot, or fresh pieces of pide (Turkish/flat bread).

HINTS: If tinned chickpeas are unavailable, soak 50 g (1¾ oz/¼ cup) dried chickpeas in cold water overnight, then drain. Place in a saucepan with water and bring to the boil. Reduce the heat and simmer for about 2½ hours, or until tender. Drain well and proceed with the recipe.

Citric acid is used in the recipes in this chapter, as it is more likely to be tolerated than lemon juice or vinegar. It can be found at some supermarkets and health food stores.

chickpea & cashew dip

Contains nuts. Free of egg, dairy, gluten and soy.

To add a delicious nutty flavour to the above dip, process 115 g (4 oz/¾ cup) cashew nuts to a smooth paste in a small food processor and add it to the chickpea mixture.

crispy wafer biscuits

These crisp wafers will put your mind at rest if you need to be certain about low-chemical snacks for your toddler. Free of egg, dairy, gluten, nut and soy.

175 g (6 oz/1 cup) rice flour

125 g (4½ oz/1 cup) cornflour (cornstarch)

40 g (1½ oz/½ cup) rice bran

2 tablespoons canola oil, plus extra for greasing

Prep time: 10 minutes
Cooking time: 25 minutes
Makes 40

To make the biscuits (crackers), preheat the oven to 200°C (400°F/Gas 6). Lightly oil two 30 x 25 cm (12 x 10 inch) Swiss roll tins (jelly roll tins).

Combine the dry ingredients in a bowl, make a well in the centre and add 185 ml (6 fl oz/¾ cup) water combined with the oil. Mix until well combined.

Divide the mixture into two portions. Press each portion of dough into a prepared tin and bake for 20–25 minutes. Allow to cool in the tin. Turn out, break into pieces and store in an airtight container for up to 2 days.

HINT: If you'd like more evenly-shaped biscuits, score the dough in the tins with a knife before you bake them, then the biscuits will easily break along the score lines once they're cooked.

vegetable soup

This soup is high in fibre and vitamins. Blend it up for a thick, easy-to-eat meal for small toddlers. Free of egg, dairy, gluten, nut and soy.

200 g (7 oz/1 cup) dried white or red beans

1 tablespoon canola oil

1 leek, halved lengthways, thickly sliced (white part only)

2 garlic cloves, crushed

400 g (14 oz) swede (rutabaga), chopped

3 celery stalks, chopped

1.5 litres (52 fl oz/6 cups) vegetable stock (see allergy-free recipe on page 238)

210 g (7½ oz/1⅔ cups) green beans, trimmed and sliced

gluten-free bread, to serve

Prep time: 15 minutes + overnight soaking

Cooking time: 1 hour 20 minutes

Serves 4–6

Wash the beans and then cover them with water and leave to soak overnight. Drain well.

Heat the oil in a large saucepan over medium heat. Cook the leek, stirring occasionally, for 4–5 minutes, or until soft. Add the garlic, swede and celery and cook for 2–3 minutes.

Add the drained beans and stock to the pan and bring to the boil. Simmer, partially covered, for 50–60 minutes, or until the beans are tender. Add the green beans and cook for a further 5–10 minutes, or until the green beans are tender. Serve with gluten-free bread.

fish patties

A good source of protein for growing toddlers, fish's omega-3 fats are also good brain food. Free of egg, dairy, gluten, nut and soy.

700 g (1 lb 9 oz) white-skinned potatoes, quartered

2 tablespoons canola oil

500 g (1 lb 2 oz) boneless white fish fillets

1 leek, halved lengthways, chopped (white part only)

2 garlic cloves, crushed

30 g (1 oz/¼ cup) chopped spring onions (scallions)

iceberg lettuce leaves, to serve

pear chutney (see page 231), to serve

Prep time: 20 minutes + 1 hour chilling
Cooking time: 25 minutes
Serves 4

Put the potato in a large saucepan. Cover with cold water and bring to the boil. Boil for 15 minutes, or until the potato is tender. Drain well. Mash with a potato masher or a fork.

Meanwhile, heat 2 teaspoons of the oil in a large non-stick frying pan over medium heat. Add the fish fillets and cook for 3–4 minutes on each side, or until cooked. Set aside to cool.

Flake the fish with a fork. Heat another 2 teaspoons of the oil in the same frying pan over medium heat. Cook the leek and garlic, stirring often, for 5–6 minutes, or until the leek softens. Set aside on a plate. Wipe the pan clean with paper towels.

Combine the mashed potato, flaked fish, leek mixture and spring onion in a large bowl and mix thoroughly. Shape into eight patties and put on a plate. Cover and refrigerate for 1 hour.

Heat the remaining oil in the frying pan over medium heat. Cook the patties for 3–4 minutes on each side, or until lightly golden and heated through. Serve with lettuce leaves and pear chutney.

continental chicken sausages

Not only are these sausages low-chemical, but they are also lower in fat and salt than most commercially-made sausages. Free of egg, dairy, gluten, nut and soy.

750 g (1 lb 10 oz) minced (ground) chicken

2 eggs, lightly beaten, or equivalent egg replacer

20 g (¾ oz/1 cup) puffed rice cereal, finely crushed

1 tablespoon finely snipped chives

1 garlic clove, crushed

2 spring onions (scallions), finely chopped

1–1.25 litres (35–44 fl oz/ 4–5 cups) chicken stock (see allergy-free recipe on page 239)

1 tablespoon canola oil

Prep time: 20 minutes + 1 hour chilling
Cooking time: 20 minutes
Serves 4

Combine the chicken, eggs or egg replacer, puffed rice, chives, garlic and spring onions in a large bowl. Using your hands, mix and knead the mixture until completely combined.

Divide the mixture into eight even portions. Using wet hands, shape each portion into a sausage shape. Put on a large plate, cover with plastic wrap and refrigerate for 1 hour.

Put the chicken stock into a large saucepan and bring to the boil. Reduce the heat and bring to a simmer. Add the sausages to the simmering stock. Cover and cook for 10–15 minutes, or until the sausages are cooked through. Remove the sausages from the stock with a slotted spoon and pat dry on paper towels.

Heat the oil in a large frying pan over medium heat and add the sausages. Cook, turning often until browned all over.

HINT: Minced (ground) chicken is available from chicken speciality shops and some supermarkets. It can be made at home by processing boneless, skinless chicken breasts or thighs.

Most commercial sausages contain preservatives. If you know a good butcher, ask to have sausages made up to your own recipe. Avoid contamination by having the sausages made at the start of the day when the machinery is clean.

chicken & carrot sausages

Free of egg, dairy, gluten, nut and soy.

Add 1 small finely grated carrot to the chicken mixture before dividing into portions, then proceed with the recipe above.

glazed drumettes

Small chicken pieces are easy-to-eat protein food for growing children and are great served as a meal or a snack. Free of egg, dairy, gluten, nut and soy.

16 chicken drumettes (see Hint)

80 ml (2½ fl oz/⅓ cup) golden syrup (dark corn syrup)

60 ml (2 fl oz/¼ cup) pear juice (see page 234)

1 tablespoon canola oil

Prep time: 20 minutes + overnight marinating

Cooking time: 25 minutes

Serves 4

Put the drumettes in a shallow non-metallic dish. Combine the remaining ingredients and pour over the drumettes, making sure they are coated all over. Marinate overnight, turning occasionally.

Preheat the oven to 180°C (350°F/Gas 4). Transfer the drumettes and marinade to a baking tin. Bake for 20–25 minutes, turning frequently during cooking and brushing with the pan juices. If the pan juices start to overbrown, add a small amount of water or stock until syrupy. Serve hot or cold.

HINT: Chicken drumettes are available from most supermarkets and chicken shops. They are simply the wing with the tip removed and the flesh scraped back away from the bone and turned inside out.

glazed chicken with garlic & poppy seeds

Free of egg, dairy, gluten, nut and soy.

For added flavour, add 2 finely chopped spring onions (scallions), 2 crushed garlic cloves and 1 tablespoon poppy seeds to the golden syrup marinade. Follow the method as above.

creamy swede purée

Swedes are a good source of potassium, as well as containing vitamin C and the B vitamin folate. Contains dairy. Free of egg, gluten, nut and soy.

600 g (1 lb 5 oz) swedes (rutabaga), thickly sliced

1 teaspoon sugar

2 tablespoons cream (whipping)

ground sea salt

Prep time: 10 minutes
Cooking time: 20 minutes
Serves 4–6

Put the swede and sugar in a saucepan and cover with cold water. Cover with a lid and bring to the boil. Reduce the heat to low and cook, for 10–15 minutes, or until the swede is tender. Drain and set aside for 5 minutes to cool.

Put the swede into a food processor and process until smooth. Stir in the cream and season with salt to taste.

Serve with grilled (broiled) lamb chops or steak.

pea purée with yoghurt

This recipe provides vitamin C and beta-carotene from the peas and calcium and phosphorus from the yoghurt. Contains dairy. Free of egg, gluten, nut and soy.

310 g (11 oz/2 cups) frozen peas

1 large handful flat-leaf (Italian) parsley, chopped

6 spring onions (scallions), chopped

125 ml (4 fl oz/½ cup) pear juice (see page 234)

½ teaspoon citric acid

250 g (9 oz/1 cup) plain yoghurt

Prep time: 10 minutes
Cooking time: 5 minutes
Serves 4

Bring a saucepan of water to the boil, then add the peas, parsley and spring onions. Cook for 2–3 minutes, or until the peas are bright green and tender.

Strain, and reserve 80 ml (2½ fl oz/⅓ cup) of the cooking liquid. Purée the pea mixture reserved cooking liquid, pear juice and citric acid in a food processor or blender. Return to the saucepan and cook over low heat until the sauce is warmed through. Remove the pan from the heat and stir in the yoghurt. Do not reheat once you have added the yoghurt or the purée will curdle.

Serve with lamb cutlets or over baked or boiled potatoes.

vegetable & veal pasta

Rich in energy-giving carbohydrate from the pasta, this recipe also provides the minerals iron, zinc and potassium, as well as vitamin C and beta-carotene. Free of egg, dairy, gluten, nut and soy.

1½ tablespoons canola oil

1 leek, halved, washed and thinly sliced (white part only)

100 g (3½ oz) swede (rutabaga), chopped

100 g (3½ oz) white-skinned potatoes, chopped

2 garlic cloves, crushed

400 g (14 oz) cabbage, core removed and shredded

500 g (1 lb 2 oz) minced (ground) lean veal

2 teaspoons cornflour (cornstarch)

375 ml (13 fl oz/1½ cups) veal stock (see allergy-free recipe on page 239)

375 g (13 oz) rice pasta

Prep time: 20 minutes

Cooking time: 25 minutes

Serves 4

Heat 1 tablespoon of the oil in a large non-stick frying pan over medium heat. Add the leek, swede and potato. Cook, stirring often, for 5–6 minutes, or until the vegetables are almost tender. Add the garlic, cabbage and 2 tablespoons water. Cover and cook for a further 7–8 minutes, or until the cabbage is tender. Remove the vegetables from the pan.

Heat the remaining oil in the pan over high heat. Add the veal and cook, stirring, for 3–4 minutes, or until well browned. Combine the cornflour with a little of the stock in a bowl, then add the remaining stock and a little salt. Add the stock mixture to the veal with the vegetables and stir until boiling. Reduce the heat and simmer for 2–3 minutes, or until the sauce thickens.

Meanwhile, cook the pasta following the packet instructions until *al dente*. Drain and return to the pan.

Divide the pasta among four serving plates. Top with the meat and vegetable mixture and serve immediately.

HINT: If your child can tolerate gluten, both pasta sauces can also be served with wheat spaghetti or other wheat pasta.

rice-crumbed fish with wedges

Rich in protein and energy-rich carbohydrates this is perfect growing food for kids. Free of egg, dairy, gluten, nut and soy.

2 eggs, or equivalent egg replacer

2 tablespoons rice drink

60 g (2¼ oz/½ cup) soy-free, gluten-free plain (all-purpose) flour

70 g (2½ oz/1 cup) rice crumbs

four 125 g (4½ oz) boneless white fish fillets

canola oil spray

iceberg lettuce leaves, to serve

pear chutney (see page 231), to serve

WEDGES

1 kg (2 lb 4 oz) white-skinned potatoes, cut into wedges

canola oil spray

Prep time: 20 minutes
Cooking time: 50 minutes
Serves 4

Preheat the oven to 220°C (425°F/Gas 7). Line two large baking trays with baking paper.

Combine the egg or egg replacer and rice drink in a shallow dish. Put the flour and rice crumbs in two separate shallow dishes. Dip the fish in the flour, then the egg mixture and lastly in the rice crumbs to coat well. Lay the crumbed fish in a single layer on one of the lined trays. Refrigerate until required.

Put the potato wedges in a large bowl. Spray the wedges with oil. Toss to coat. Spread over the other lined tray.

Bake the potato wedges for 30 minutes, turning once. Put the wedges on the lower shelf of the oven. Remove the fish from the refrigerator, then spray both sides of the fish lightly with oil. Add the fish to the top shelf and cook for 20 minutes turning halfway through, or until the fish is cooked and the wedges are crispy.

breadcrumb-coated fish

Contains egg, dairy and gluten. Free of nut and soy.

Commercial breadcrumbs always contain preservatives. You can make your own by putting preservative-free bread slices on baking trays and slowly baking until completely crisp. Process in a food processor and store in an airtight jar. To make breadcrumb-coated fish, combine 1 egg and 1 tablespoon milk in a bowl, put 60 g (2¼ oz/½ cup) plain (all-purpose) flour in a separate bowl and 165 g (5¾ oz/2 cups) home-made breadcrumbs in a third bowl. Dip the fish first in the flour, then the egg wash and lastly in the breadcrumbs. Follow the cooking method in the recipe above.

crunchy chicken bits

Low-chemical food can also be tasty and fun to eat and these chicken bits are a treat as well as being nutritious. Free of egg, dairy, gluten, nut and soy.

canola oil, for greasing

1 kg (2 lb 4 oz) boneless, skinless chicken thighs or breasts, fat removed

40 g (1½ oz/⅓ cup) soy-free, gluten-free plain (all-purpose) flour

2 eggs, or equivalent egg replacer

300 g (10½ oz) plain potato chips (crisps), crushed

Prep time: 20 minutes
Cooking time: 20 minutes
Serves 4–6

Preheat the oven to 180°C (350°F/Gas 4). Lightly grease two baking trays.

Cut the chicken into 3 cm (1¼ inch) pieces. Coat the chicken lightly in the flour, then dip in the the egg or egg replacer combined with 2 tablespoons water. Roll the chicken in the potato chips, pressing down firmly.

Lay out the chicken in a single layer on the prepared trays and bake for 15–20 minutes, or until cooked through and golden brown. Turn once during cooking.

HINT: For extra-crunchy chicken, deep-fry in hot canola oil until cooked and golden brown instead of baking.

crunchy chicken bits with chives

Free of egg, dairy, gluten, nut and soy.

Add 15 g (½ oz/¼ cup) finely snipped chives to the potato chips. Follow the cooking method in the recipe above.

crunchy chicken bits with garlic

Free of egg, dairy, gluten, nut and soy.

Fry 1–2 crushed garlic cloves in a small amount of canola oil until lightly golden. Cool, then add to the potato chips. Follow the cooking method in the recipe above.

chickpea fritters

These fritters are an excellent source of fibre and provide good amounts of protein and iron too. Free of egg, dairy, gluten, nut and soy.

2 tablespoons canola oil

4 spring onions (scallions), sliced

2 garlic cloves, chopped

600 g (1 lb 5 oz) tinned chickpeas, rinsed and drained

1 egg, or equivalent egg replacer

pear chutney (see page 231), to serve

small cos (romaine) lettuce leaves, to serve

crusty gluten-free bread, to serve

Prep time: 20 minutes
Cooking time: 10 minutes
Makes 6

Heat 2 teaspoons of the oil in a large non-stick frying pan over medium heat. Add the spring onions and garlic and cook, stirring, for 1–2 minutes, or until the spring onion softens.

Put the chickpeas and spring onion mixture in a food processor. Process until the mixture starts to hold together. Transfer to a bowl and mix in the egg or egg replacer. Using your hands, shape the mixture into six even fritters.

Heat the remaining oil in a large non-stick frying pan over medium heat. Add the chickpea fritters (cook in two batches if necessary) and cook for 2 minutes on each side, or until golden. Serve with chutney, lettuce and crusty gluten-free bread.

pear & bean salad

This salad is rich in protein, fibre, the minerals iron and zinc as well as vitamins. Free of egg, dairy, gluten, nut and soy.

4 tinned pear halves, drained and chopped

40 g (1½ oz/½ cup) mung bean sprouts

60 g (2¼ oz/½ cup) sliced, cooked green beans

4 spring onions (scallions), chopped

100 g (3½ oz/½ cup) cooked kidney beans

100 g (3½ oz/½ cup) cooked soya beans

1 tablespoon poppy seeds

DRESSING

60 ml (2 fl oz/¼ cup) canola oil

¾ teaspoon citric acid

½ teaspoon sugar

1 garlic clove, crushed

Prep time: 15 minutes

Cooking time: Nil

Serves 4–6

Combine the pear, mung bean sprouts, green beans, spring onions, kidney beans and soya beans in a large bowl. Mix together gently.

To make the dressing, combine the oil, citric acid, sugar, garlic and 60 ml (2 fl oz/¼ cup) water. Pour over the vegetables and stir to mix through. Chill before serving. Sprinkle with the poppy seeds just before serving.

HINT: This salad is best made the day before serving to allow the full combination of flavours. Use any combination of your toddler's favourite beans or use tinned mixed beans.

sausage rolls

Using healthy fats and natural ingredients these sausage rolls will be a nutritious snack any time. Free of egg, dairy, gluten, nut and soy.

canola oil, for greasing

400 g (14 oz) white-skinned potatoes, roughly chopped

1 tablespoon canola oil

125 g (4½ oz/1 cup) soy-free, gluten-free self-raising flour

½ teaspoon gluten-free baking powder

½ teaspoon ground sea salt

1 egg, or equivalent egg replacer

FILLING

300 g (10½ oz) minced (ground) chicken or veal

1 egg, or equivalent egg replacer

40 g (1½ oz/½ cup) gluten-free fresh breadcrumbs

1 spring onion (scallion), finely chopped

½ teaspoon ground sea salt

1 egg, or equivalent egg replacer, for brushing

Prep time: 45 minutes
Cooking time: 25 minutes
Makes 18

Preheat the oven to 200°C (400°F/Gas 6). Lightly grease two baking trays. Boil or steam the potato for 15 minutes, or until tender. Drain and return to the pan and mash until smooth. You will need about 235 g (8½ oz/1 cup) mashed potato for this recipe.

Combine the mashed potato and oil in a large bowl. Add the sifted dry ingredients and enough egg to mix to a smooth dough. Knead on a lightly floured work surface until smooth. Roll the dough out into a 35 cm (14 inch) square, trimming the edges. Cut the dough evenly into three strips.

To make the filling, combine the meat, egg or egg replacer, breadcrumbs, spring onion and salt in a bowl. Add 1 tablespoon water and mix well to combine. Divide the filling into three portions and, using wet hands, form each portion into thin rolls. Lay the filling along the centre of the pastry strips and brush the extra egg along the edges. Wrap the pastry around the filling, placing them seam side down. Repeat with the remaining filling and pastry.

Brush the rolls with the remaining egg, then cut each roll into six pieces. Place the sausage rolls on the prepared trays, prick the tops with a fork and bake for 20–25 minutes, or until cooked through and lightly browned.

HINTS: Sausage rolls can be made a day in advance and kept in the refrigerator. When required, wrap the cooked sausage rolls in foil and reheat at 180°C (350°F/Gas 4) for 5–8 minutes. If your child can tolerate gluten, you can use commercial puff pastry with no added preservatives or antioxidants, instead of potato pastry.

gluten-free pear muffins

With gluten-free flours available in most supermarkets, home-made muffins like these are easy to make. Free of egg, dairy, gluten, nut and soy.

canola oil, for greasing

250 g (9 oz/2 cups) soy-free, gluten-free self-raising flour

2 teaspoons gluten-free baking powder

140 g (5 oz/¾ cup) soft brown sugar

170 ml (5½ fl oz/⅔ cup) rice drink

80 ml (2½ fl oz/⅓ cup) canola oil

2 eggs, or equivalent egg replacer

2 ripe pears (about 450 g/ 1 lb), peeled, cored and mashed

Prep time: 15 minutes
Cooking time: 20 minutes
Makes 12

Preheat the oven to 180°C (350°F/Gas 4). Lightly grease a 12-hole muffin tin with canola oil.

Sift the flour and baking powder into a large bowl and add the sugar. In a separate bowl, combine the rice drink, oil and eggs or egg replacer. Add the rice drink mixture and pears to the flour mixture. Use a large metal spoon to mix until just combined. Spoon the mixture into the muffin tin.

Bake for 18–20 minutes, or until a skewer inserted in the centre comes out clean. Leave for 5 minutes before turning onto a wire rack.

HINT: These muffins need to be eaten the day they are made.

gluten-free banana muffins

Free of egg, dairy, gluten, nut and soy.

Replace the pears with 2 large, ripe bananas, mashed.

gluten-free rhubarb muffins

Freee of egg, dairy, gluten, nut and soy.

Replace the pears with ½ bunch rhubarb, washed and cut into 2 cm (¾ inch) long pieces. Increase the rice drink to 185 ml (6 fl oz/¾ cup).

cupcakes

This recipe will make a gluten- and egg-free celebration so much easier to achieve. Free of egg, dairy, gluten, nut and soy.

125 g (4½ oz) dairy-free margarine

115 g (4 oz/½ cup) caster (superfine) sugar

2 eggs, or equivalent egg replacer

125 g (4½ oz/1 cup) soy-free, gluten-free self-raising flour

90 g (3¼ oz/½ cup) rice flour

3 teaspoons gluten-free baking powder

125 ml (4 fl oz/½ cup) rice drink

icing (confectioners') sugar, for dusting

Prep time: 15 minutes
Cooking time: 20 minutes
Makes 24

Preheat the oven to 180°C (350°F/Gas 4). Line two 12-hole muffin tins with paper cases.

Using an electric mixer, beat the margarine and sugar together well until light and fluffy. Add the eggs or egg replacer, one at a time, beating well after each addition.

Fold in the sifted dry ingredients alternately with the rice drink.

Spoon the mixture evenly into the muffin holes and bake for about 15–20 minutes, or until a skewer comes out clean when inserted into the centre.

Dust the cupcakes with icing sugar.

Hyperactive children can find the natural chemicals in so-called healthy foods just as much of a problem as artificial additives. In sensitive children, adverse effects are dose-related and can build up over a period of time, especially when the chemicals are eaten in many other different foods.

gluten-free pikelets

If dairy is allowed, serve these pikelets with pear yoghurt to make a calcium- and carbohydrate-rich snack. Contains egg. Free of dairy, gluten, nut and soy.

85 g (3 oz/⅔ cup) soy-free, gluten-free plain (all-purpose) flour

½ teaspoon bicarbonate of soda (baking soda)

1 teaspoon cream of tartar

30 g (1 oz/⅓ cup) rice bran

2 eggs, separated

1 tablespoon canola oil

canola oil spray, for greasing

pear jam (see page 235), for serving (optional)

Prep time: 15 minutes

Cooking time: 15 minutes

Makes about 24

To make the pikelets (griddle cakes), sift the flour, bicarbonate of soda and cream of tartar into a bowl. Mix in the rice bran. Make a well in the centre and stir in the combined egg yolks, oil and 250 ml (9 fl oz/1 cup) water. Beat well until smooth.

Beat the egg whites until stiff peaks form, then fold into the batter using a large metal spoon.

Spray a non-stick frying pan lightly with oil and place over medium heat. Place 2 tablespoons of the mixture for each pikelet in the pan, allowing room for spreading. When the mixture starts to set and the bubbles burst, turn over and brown the other side. Repeat the process with the remaining mixture. Place the pikelets on a wire cake rack to cool. Serve with pear jam, if desired.

HINT: Pikelets can be frozen and reheated briefly in a warm oven.

pikelets with pear yoghurt

Contains egg, dairy and gluten. Free of nut and soy.

Replace the gluten-free flour with regular plain (all-purpose) flour. You will need between 185–250 ml (6–9 fl oz/¾–1 cup) water. Serve with pear yoghurt. To make, combine 250 g (9 oz/1 cup) plain yoghurt, ½ peeled and chopped pear and 2 teaspoons soft brown sugar.

carob milkshake

This milkshake is rich in calcium and phosphorus, excellent for strong bones and teeth. Contains dairy. Free of egg, gluten, nut and soy.

1 tablespoon carob powder

1 tablespoon sugar

500 ml (17 fl oz/2 cups) milk, well chilled

40 g (1½ oz/¼ cup) finely chopped carob buttons

Prep time: 5 minutes

Cooking time: Nil

Serves 2

Dissolve the carob powder and sugar in 1 tablespoon hot water. Allow to cool.

Combine the milk and carob mixture by whisking or beating together. Pour into long glasses. Top with finely chopped carob buttons.

HINT: Ask your health food store whether their carob buttons contain dairy and/or soy.

mayonnaise

Young children on restricted diets due to an allergy or intolerance may struggle to gain weight. Condiments like this with lots of healthy fat can help them out. Contains egg. Free of dairy, gluten, nut and soy.

2 egg yolks
¼ teaspoon ground sea salt
250 ml (9 fl oz/1 cup) canola oil
¼ teaspoon citric acid

Prep time: 20 minutes
Cooking time: Nil
Makes 250 g (9 oz/1 cup)

Put the egg yolks and salt in a bowl and whisk together until well combined and thick.

Gradually whisk in the oil, drop by drop until a quarter of the oil has been added. The mixture should be thick at this stage. Very slowly pour in the remaining oil in a thin steady stream, whisking continuously. Beat in the citric acid. Store the mayonnaise in a sterilized glass jar in the refrigerator for up to 3 days.

HINT: Mayonnaise can be made in a blender or food processor. Use the same ingredients as above. Blend the eggs and salt for a few seconds. With the motor running, pour in the oil in a steady thin stream. When all the oil has been added, the mixture should be thick.

pear chutney

Foods with lots of flavour are often the ones food-sensitive kids can't have. This recipe is an exception. Free of egg, dairy, gluten, nut and soy.

820 g (1 lb 13 oz) tinned pear halves in syrup

125 g (4½ oz/⅔ cup) soft brown sugar

1½ teaspoons citric acid

1 teaspoon ground sea salt

Prep time: 10 minutes

Cooking time: 25 minutes

Makes 375 g (13 oz/1½ cups)

Drain and chop the pears, reserving the syrup.

Pour the syrup into a saucepan. Bring to the boil and boil until the mixture is reduced by half.

Add the pears, sugar, citric acid and salt. Reduce the heat. Allow to simmer for about 10–15 minutes, or until the mixture is thick.

Spoon into hot, sterilized jars. Seal, label and date. Once opened, store in the refrigerator and use within 3 weeks.

pear slushy

Here is a safe and sweet treat for toddlers on long hot days. Free of egg, dairy, gluten, nut and soy.

825 g (1 lb 13 oz) tinned pear halves in syrup

1 teaspoon citric acid

Prep time: 15 minutes + freezing time

Cooking time: Nil

Serves 4–6

Put the pears, their syrup and the citric acid into a blender. Blend on high for 2–3 minutes.

Pour into a shallow metal tin and freeze for about 1 hour, or until just frozen around the edges. Scrape the ice back into the mixture with a fork. Repeat every 30 minutes until the mixture consists of even-sized ice crystals. Serve immediately or beat with a fork and refreeze until just before serving. Allow to soften slightly in the refrigerator before using. The mixture should be slushy.

Pile into long cups and serve with a spoon and a straw.

fried flat bread

This recipe helps to fill the need for hard-to-find starchy snacks for toddlers with wheat or gluten intolerance. Free of egg, dairy, gluten, nut and soy.

135 g (4¾ oz/¾ cup) rice flour

135 g (4¾ oz/¾ cup) potato flour (see Hints)

1 teaspoon gluten-free baking powder

1 teaspoon ground sea salt

1 tablespoon canola oil, plus extra, for frying

185–250 ml (6–9 fl oz/ ¾–1 cup) warm water

Prep time: 10 minutes

Cooking time: 25 minutes

Makes 8 rounds

Sift the rice flour, potato flour and baking powder into a large bowl. Add the salt. Make a well in the centre and add the oil. Gradually stir in enough water until a thick batter is formed.

Heat 1 cm (½ inch) oil in a frying pan over medium–high heat. Pour in enough batter to form a round about 10–12 cm (4–5 inches) across. Fry until golden brown, then turn and brown the other side. Drain on paper towels. Repeat with the remaining batter. Add more oil to the pan as needed, ensuring it is heated through before use.

HINTS: Potato flour is often preserved with sulphite, but most of it will disappear during the cooking process. Use this bread as an accompaniment to any meat or lentil dish or top with your toddler's favourite food.

pear juice

This juice is easy to digest and a great source of fibre. It is best if diluted with equal parts of water for toddlers. Free of egg, dairy, gluten, nut and soy.

820 g (1 lb 13 oz) tinned pear halves in syrup

Prep time: 5 minutes
Cooking time: Nil
Serves 4–6

Put the pears and syrup into a blender. Blend on high speed for 2–3 minutes, or until puréed.

Scoop the pear juice into a covered container and store in the refrigerator for up to 4 days.

HINT: Pear juice may be diluted with unflavoured mineral water or cooled, boiled tap water. Pear juice can also be used to naturally sweeten breakfast cereals such as porridge or muesli (granola).

mango juice

This delicious juice is also an excellent source of beta-carotene — a nutrient that converts to vitamin A in the body. Free of egg, dairy, gluten, nut and soy.

550 g (1 lb 4 oz) fresh mango, peeled
55 g (2 oz/¼ cup) sugar
125 ml (4 fl oz/½ cup) water

Prep time: 5 minutes
Cooking time: Nil
Serves 4–6

Blend the mango flesh with the sugar and water in a blender on high speed for 2–3 minutes, or until puréed.

Dilute as desired to serve.

HINT: If fresh mangoes aren't in season, use 680 g (1 lb 8 oz) tinned mangoes in syrup and blend to a purée — you won't need any extra sugar or water. Dilute as desired.

pear jam

When your toddler's food choices are restricted, it is nice to be able to offer a sweet choice to spread on bread. Free of egg, dairy, gluten, nut and soy.

750 g (1 lb 10 oz) ripe, peeled pears, or 1.6 kg (3 lb 8 oz) tinned pears, drained

750 g (1 lb 10 oz/3⅓ cups) sugar

50 g (1¾ oz) jam setting mixture

Prep time: 10 minutes

Cooking time: 10 minutes

Makes about 785 g (1 lb 11 oz/2⅓ cups)

Purée the pears in a blender or food processor. Scoop the purée into a large saucepan and heat over medium heat. Stir in the sugar and jam setting mixture. Reduce the heat to low and stir until the sugar is dissolved. Increase the heat and bring to the boil. Boil for 5 minutes, stirring occasionally, then remove from the heat.

Allow to cool for 10 minutes, then pour into sterilized jars. Seal, label and date. Once opened, store in the refrigerator and use within 4 weeks.

HINT: Use as a spread, filling or topping.

When you have time to spare, the preparation of a few of the basics will stand you in good stead for those occasions when you haven't the time but want healthy and tasty food. Low-salt stocks mean quick-to-make soups, a good white sauce can rescue many a plain meal while our basic tomato sauce can be used for more than just a good pasta sauce.

basics

vegetable stock

Commercial stocks are high in salt and not suitable to include in food you prepare for your toddler or baby. This recipe lets you preserve the natural tastes of vegetables without added salt.

1 tablespoon oil

1 onion, chopped

2 leeks, thickly sliced (white part only)

4 carrots, chopped

2 parsnips, chopped

4 celery stalks, leaves included, chopped

2 bay leaves

1 bouquet garni (see Hint)

4 unpeeled garlic cloves

8 black peppercorns

Prep time: 20 minutes

Cooking time: 1½ hours

Makes: 2.5 litres (87 fl oz/ 10 cups)

Heat the oil in a large, heavy-based saucepan and add the onion, leek, carrot, parsnip and celery. Cover and cook for 5 minutes without colouring. Add 3 litres (105 fl oz/12 cups) water. Bring to the boil. Add the bay leaves, bouquet garni, garlic and peppercorns. Reduce the heat to low and simmer for 1 hour. Skim the froth from the surface of the stock regularly.

Strain the stock. Set aside to cool, then transfer to an airtight container. Store in the refrigerator for up to 2 days or in the freezer for up to 6 months.

HINT: To make your own bouquet garni, tie together with a string or wrap in a piece of cheesecloth (muslin) 4 sprigs parsley or chervil, 1 sprig fresh thyme and 1 bay leaf.

allergy-free vegetable stock

Heat 1 tablespoon canola oil in a large saucepan over medium heat. Add 3 sliced celery stalks, 350 g (12 oz) chopped swede (rutabaga), 1 large leek, halved lengthways and chopped, and 3 crushed garlic cloves. Cook, stirring often, for 5–8 minutes, or until the vegetables turn a light gold. Pour in 4.5 litres (157 fl oz/18 cups) water. Cover with a lid and bring to the boil. Simmer, partially covered, for 1½ hours, skimming the froth from the surface of the stock regularly. Strain the stock. Set aside to cool, then transfer to an airtight container. Store in the refrigerator for up to 2 days or in the freezer for up to 6 months. Makes 2.5 litres (87 fl oz/10 cups).

chicken stock

This recipe makes a flavoursome stock for soups and casseroles without the added extras of many commercial varieties.

2 kg (4 lb 8 oz) chicken bones

2 unpeeled onions, quartered

2 unpeeled carrots, chopped

2 celery stalks, leaves included, chopped

1 bouquet garni

12 black peppercorns

Prep time: 20 minutes

Cooking time: 3 hours 10 minutes

Makes: 2.5 litres (87 fl oz/ 10 cups)

Put the chicken bones, onion, carrot, celery and 3.5 litres (122 fl oz/ 14 cups) water in a large, heavy-based saucepan. Bring slowly to the boil. Skim the surface as required and add the bouquet garni and peppercorns. Reduce the heat to low and simmer gently for 3 hours. Skim the froth from the surface regularly.

Strain the stock. Set aside to cool, then refrigerate until cold. Spoon off any fat that has set on the surface. Transfer to an airtight container. Store in the refrigerator for up to 2 days or in the freezer for up to 6 months.

allergy-free chicken or veal stock

Put 500 g (1 lb 2 oz) chicken or veal bones in a large heavy-based saucepan. Add 1 leek, 1 celery stalk and 1 carrot, all roughly chopped, and 4 parsley stalks (without foliage). Cover with water and bring to the boil, skimming the surface. Reduce the heat and simmer for about 1–1½ hours, uncovered. Strain through a colander, then through a fine sieve. Remove any fat from the surface. Store in the refrigerator for up to 2 days or in the freezer for up to 6 months. Makes about 500 ml (17 fl oz/2 cups).

beef stock

Full of the flavour and goodness of meaty bones, this stock will enrich any recipe you use it in.

2 kg (4 lb 8 oz) beef bones

2 unpeeled carrots, chopped

2 unpeeled onions, quartered

2 tablespoons tomato paste (conentrated purée)

2 celery stalks, leaves included, chopped

1 bouquet garni

12 black peppercorns

Prep time: 20 minutes

Cooking time: 4 hours 50 minutes

Makes about 1.75 litres (61 fl oz/7 cups)

Preheat the oven to 210°C (415°F/Gas 6–7). Put the bones in a baking tin and bake for 30 minutes, turning occasionally. Add the carrot and onion and cook for a further 20 minutes. Allow to cool.

Put the bones, onion and carrot in a large, heavy-based saucepan. Drain the excess fat from the baking tin and pour 250 ml (9 fl oz/1 cup) water into the tin. Stir to dissolve any pan juices, then add the liquid to the pan.

Add the tomato paste, celery and 2.5 litres (87 fl oz/10 cups) water. Bring to the boil, skimming the surface as required, and then add the bouquet garni and peppercorns. Reduce the heat to low and simmer gently for 4 hours. Skim the froth from the surface regularly.

Strain through a colander, then through a fine sieve. Remove any fat from the surface. Store in the refrigerator for up to 2 days or in the freezer for up to 6 months.

basic tomato sauce

Keep this sauce on hand stored in small portions in the freezer. It is perfect for a quick pasta meal or use it to top vegetables, rice or poultry dishes.

1.5 kg (3 lb 5 oz) tomatoes
1 tablespoon olive oil
1 onion, finely chopped
2 garlic cloves, crushed
2 tablespoons tomato paste (concentrated purée)
1 teaspoon dried oregano
1 teaspoon dried basil
1 teaspoon sugar

Prep time: 25 minutes
Cooking time: 25 minutes
Serves 4

Score a cross on the base of each tomato, place in a bowl of boiling water for 10 seconds, then plunge into cold water and peel away the skin from the cross. Finely chop the flesh.

Heat the oil in pan. Add the onion and cook, stirring, over medium heat for 3 minutes, or until soft. Add the garlic and cook for 1 minute. Add the tomato, tomato paste, oregano, basil and sugar. Bring to the boil, then reduce the heat and simmer for 20 minutes, or until the sauce has thickened slightly.

Store in an airtight container in the refrigerator for up to 2 days or in the freezer for up to 6 months.

white sauce

A basic white sauce is a wonderfully adaptable food for young children and a good way to include dairy in the diet of the reluctant milk drinker.

250 ml (9 fl oz/1 cup) milk
1 onion slice
1 bay leaf
6 peppercorns
30 g (1 oz) unsalted butter
1 tablespoon plain (all-purpose) flour

Prep time: 15 minutes
Cooking time: 10 minutes
Serves 2–4

Put the milk, onion, bay leaf and peppercorns in a small saucepan. Bring to the boil, remove from the heat and leave to infuse for 10 minutes. Strain the milk, discarding the flavourings.

Melt the butter in a small pan and stir in the flour. Cook, stirring, for 1 minute until the mixture is golden and bubbling. Remove from the heat and gradually add the milk, stirring until completely smooth. Return to the heat and stir until the mixture boils. Continue cooking for 1 minute, or until thick. Remove from the heat and serve.

cheese sauce

To make a basic cheese sauce, add 60 g (2¼ oz/½ cup) finely grated cheddar cheese to the white sauce when removed from the heat. Stir the cheese through until melted, then serve.

barbecue dipping sauce

Something to dip food into is always a favourite with toddlers. Choose a salt-reduced ketchup and this recipe will be a good accompaniment to finger foods.

2 teaspoons oil
I small onion, finely chopped
I tablespoon malt vinegar
I tablespoon soft brown sugar
80 ml (2½ fl oz/⅓ cup) salt-reduced tomato sauce (ketchup)
I tablespoon worcestershire sauce

Prep time: 15 minutes
Cooking time: 10 minutes
Serves 2–4

Heat the oil in a small saucepan and cook the onion over low heat for 3 minutes, or until soft, stirring occasionally.

Add the remaining ingredients and bring to the boil. Reduce the heat and simmer for 3 minutes, stirring occasionally. Serve warm or at room temperature. Can be kept covered and refrigerated, for up to 1 week.

Having the right tools can make feeding your baby much easier. This section includes tips on cooking utensils and feeding equipment. Plus, with all the nutrition information parents are bombarded with, it can be easy to lose sight of the bigger, and much simpler, picture. So we have also provided you with a healthy diet pyramid to cut to the core of what you are trying to achieve when you prepare family meals.

useful information
& index

necessary equipment

KITCHEN EQUIPMENT

You will probably find that you already have most of the things you need to make and store baby food if you already cook frequently:

• *Sieve and/or blender for making purées.*

• *Steamer for cooking vegetables, fish and poultry.*

• *Ice cube containers for freezing and storing food.*

As with most items specifically designed for babies, you can spend a lot of money on eating equipment. However, this is not necessary. Your baby will only need one or two bowls and several flat spoons — you can add a baby fork at a later date. You will also want a few bibs, so you can wash or soak some while your baby is wearing others. The ideal bib covers your baby's shoulders and stomach. Several baby cups with non-spill features will be extremely useful as your baby learns that the drink is supposed to go into his tummy, not on the floor, the highchair, or on your lap. If you have sterilizing equipment for bottles, you can add baby spoons and beaker spouts to the mix. Otherwise, cleaning them carefully and thoroughly in hot soapy water, then rinsing them just as thoroughly should get them clean. Using the dishwasher to clean baby's bowls and utensils is also fine. You may also want to consider a mess mat, which will also need to be cleaned at the end of every meal.

choosing a highchair

A highchair is a major piece of equipment. There are safety and ease-of-use issues with highchairs so look for one that:

• Has a five-point harness to prevent your child from falling or climbing out.

• Is strong but not too heavy for you to lift. Lean on it to check its strength.

• Has no sharp edges and is without removable pieces that could find their way into your child's mouth.

• Fits into your kitchen, family room or around your table. If the legs stick out will you trip over them?

• Has a tray that is well secured when in place, but can be easily removed for cleaning.

• Can be adjusted for height. Also, check if the seat reclines — not all highchairs recline, but this mechanism can be useful when you have a young baby. Any adjustment knobs should be out of a child's reach when they are sitting in the highchair.

• Folds away easily, ideally with one hand. If space is a problem, folding it up quickly and easily being able to lift it will be important.

• Has an adjustable leg rest for your child.

• Is reasonably easy to wipe down.

the healthy diet pyramid for the whole family

EAT LEAST
sugar, fats and oils, salt

EAT IN MODERATION
eggs, dairy products and
alternatives, meat, poultry, fish,
seafood and nuts

EAT MOST
grains and cereal products,
fruits, vegetables, legumes

SENSES	FIRST WEEKS	2 MONTHS	3 MONTHS	4 MONTHS	5 MONTHS	6 MONTHS
REACTIONS	6–8 weeks: first social smiles			Likes to be handled	Enjoys new tastes	May start to cling
HEARING AND SPEECH	Hears from birth. Cries from hunger and discomfort	Gurgling 'oos' and 'ahs'	Brief attention to sounds including voices. Searches for sounds with eyes	Usually disturbed by angry voices. May utter sounds when spoken to or pleased. More consonants		Turns to sounds. Chuckles and babbles
SIGHT	Looks briefly at bright or close objects	Following with eyes	Looking at faces and objects for longer periods of time		Recognizes everyday objects, e.g. a cup. Watches hands	Watches adults across the room
HAND MOVEMENTS			Holds objects which are placed in hands for short time	Reaching out to get objects		Objects put into mouth
BODY MOVEMENTS AND GETTING ABOUT	When placed on stomach will turn head to side. Movements are jerky		Can hold head steady for a period of time. When baby propped in sitting position, head tends to bob forward	Can hold head and chest up when lying on stomach, taking weight on forearms		Lifts head to look at feet. Sits with support. 6–8 months: rolling over

8 MONTHS	9 MONTHS	10 MONTHS	12 MONTHS	15 MONTHS	18 MONTHS	2 YEARS
May cry when a parent goes out of sight. This may last past second birthday	Shy of strangers. Can cling to parents and hide face	Reacts to praise. Understands 'no'		Dependant on adult's presence. Active and curious. Starting to explore. Emotionally 'up and down'	Exploring energetically. Plays alone, but likes to be near adult. Emotionally still dependent on familiar adults	Constantly seeks attention. Clings tightly in affection, fear or fatigue. Tantrums when frustrated
Practising different sounds, e.g. 'googoo' and 'adada'	Smacks lips together and may start to imitate adult noises, e.g. 'brr'		Understands some words and phrases. First words with meaning about this time, e.g. 'dada', 'mama'	Starting to understand and obey simple commands such as 'get your shoes'. Using a few true words	Using both noises and pointing to indicate what they want. Number of words increased	Speech becoming clearer. Puts two or more words together to form simple phrases, e.g. 'go shop'
Sees small beads		Looks for objects dropped out of sight and finds toys hidden under a blanket		Enjoys picture books. Points at named objects		Notices details in picture books. Recognizes familiar adults in photographs once they are pointed out
7–8 months: able to transfer an object from one hand to another		Beginning to use index finger and thumb to pick up small objects		Picks up a lot of small objects using finger and thumb. Can throw things quite forcibly (this is still a game)	Can turn pages of book one at a time	Scribbles lines and rough circles. Feeds self with spoon
	9–10 months: sits alone on floor for 10–15 minutes. Props to side or forwards to balance. Attempts to crawl (some children get around by bottom shuffling or wriggling and may walk later — up to 18 months). 10–18 months: first steps		Pulls self to standing position and lets self down again holding onto furniture	Can climb on furniture	Around this time can usually walk quite well. Runs (with falls). Can climb stairs	Starting to kick and can throw a ball. Very mobile and active

First produced by the Paediatric Health Education Unit, University of Sydney

index

Published by Murdoch Books Pty Limited.

Chief Executive: Juliet Rogers
Publisher: Kay Scarlett

Editorial Director: Diana Hill
Project Manager: Paul McNally
Design Concept and Design: Susanne Geppert
Editor: Ariana Klepac
Food Editor: Rebecca Truda
Nutritional consultant: Karen Kingham
Photographer: Ian Hofstetter
Stylist: Jane Collins
Food preparation: Joanne Kelly
Recipes: Rebecca Truda and members of the Murdoch Books Test Kitchen.
Production: Monika Paratore

National Library of Australia Cataloguing-in-Publication Data: Fallows, Carol. Baby & toddler food: recipes and practical information for feeding babies and toddlers. Includes index. ISBN 1 74045 501 0. 1. Cookery (Baby foods) 2. Toddlers — Nutrition. 3. Baby foods. I. Title. (Series: Food for life) 641.56222.

Murdoch Books Australia
Pier 8/9, 23 Hickson Road
Millers Point NSW 2000
Phone: + 61 (0) 2 8220 2000 Fax: + 61 (0) 2 8220 2558

Murdoch Books UK Ltd
Erico House, 6th Floor North, 93–99 Upper Richmond Road
Putney, London SW15 2TG
Phone: + 44 (0) 20 8785 5995   Fax +44 (0) 20 8785 5985

IMPORTANT: Those who might be at risk from the effects of salmonella food poisoning (the elderly, pregnant women, young children and those suffering from immune deficiency diseases) should consult their doctor with any concerns about eating raw eggs.

CONVERSION GUIDE: You may find cooking times vary depending on the oven you are using. For fan-forced ovens, as a general rule, set the oven temperature to 20°C (70°F) lower than indicated in the recipe. We have used 20 ml (4 teaspoon) tablespoon measures. If you are using a 15 ml (3 teaspoon) tablespoon, for most recipes the difference will not be noticeable. However, for recipes using baking powder, gelatine, bicarbonate of soda, small amounts of flour and cornflour (cornstarch), add an extra teaspoon for each tablespoon specified.

The Publisher thanks Dinosaur Designs, Mud Australia, Bison Homewares and IKEA for assistance in the photography of this book.